MODERN BUSINESS MANAGEMENT

CREATING A BUILT-TO-CHANGE ORGANIZATION

Doug Dockery

Laureen Knudsen

technologies

CA Press

Apress®

Modern Business Management: Creating a Built-to-Change Organization

Doug Dockery
Plano, Texas, USA

Laureen Knudsen
Escondido, California, USA

ISBN-13 (pbk): 978-1-4842-3260-6
https://doi.org/10.1007/978-1-4842-3261-3

ISBN-13 (electronic): 978-1-4842-3261-3

Library of Congress Control Number: 2017961846

Managing Director: Welmoed Spahr
Editorial Director: Todd Green
Acquisitions Editor: Susan McDermott
Development Editor: Laura Berendson
Technical Reviewer: Rick Langsford
Coordinating Editor: Rita Fernando
Copy Editor: Teresa Horton

Distributed to the book trade worldwide by Springer Science+Business Media New York, 233 Spring Street, 6th Floor, New York, NY 10013. Phone 1-800-SPRINGER, fax (201) 348-4505, e-mail orders-ny@springer-sbm.com, or visit www.springeronline.com. Apress Media, LLC is a California LLC and the sole member (owner) is Springer Science + Business Media Finance Inc (SSBM Finance Inc). SSBM Finance Inc is a **Delaware** corporation.

For information on translations, please e-mail rights@apress.com, or visit http://www.apress.com/rights-permissions.

Apress titles may be purchased in bulk for academic, corporate, or promotional use. eBook versions and licenses are also available for most titles. For more information, reference our Print and eBook Bulk Sales web page at http://www.apress.com/bulk-sales.

Any source code or other supplementary material referenced by the author in this book is available to readers on GitHub via the book's product page, located at www.apress.com/9781484232606. For more detailed information, please visit http://www.apress.com/source-code.

Printed on acid-free paper

Apress Business: The Unbiased Source of Business Information

Apress business books provide essential information and practical advice, each written for practitioners by recognized experts. Busy managers and professionals in all areas of the business world—and at all levels of technical sophistication—look to our books for the actionable ideas and tools they need to solve problems, update and enhance their professional skills, make their work lives easier, and capitalize on opportunity.

Whatever the topic on the business spectrum—entrepreneurship, finance, sales, marketing, management, regulation, information technology, among others—Apress has been praised for providing the objective information and unbiased advice you need to excel in your daily work life. Our authors have no axes to grind; they understand they have one job only—to deliver up-to-date, accurate information simply, concisely, and with deep insight that addresses the real needs of our readers.

It is increasingly hard to find information—whether in the news media, on the Internet, and now all too often in books—that is even-handed and has your best interests at heart. We therefore hope that you enjoy this book, which has been carefully crafted to meet our standards of quality and unbiased coverage.

We are always interested in your feedback or ideas for new titles. Perhaps you'd even like to write a book yourself. Whatever the case, reach out to us at editorial@apress.com and an editor will respond swiftly. Incidentally, at the back of this book, you will find a list of useful related titles. Please visit us at www.apress.com to sign up for newsletters and discounts on future purchases.

The Apress Business Team

Contents

About the Authors vii

About the Technical Reviewer ix

Acknowledgments. xi

Introduction xiii

Chapter 1:   Agile?   1

Chapter 2:   My Contrarian View   17

Chapter 3:   Where's My Flying Car?   45

Chapter 4:   Three Simple Questions.   57

Chapter 5:   Houston, We Have a Chasm   71

Chapter 6:   Introducing the Modern Business   105

Chapter 7:   But Where Is My Value?   123

Chapter 8:   True Transformation Equals Value   133

Chapter 9:   How Do You Know It's Working?   145

Index   153

About the Authors

Doug Dockery is an architect of Agile solutions and has served as an Enterprise Agile Coach with extensive experience in leading Agile transformations. Doug has led transformations and worked directly with companies in the *Fortune* 100 to adopt true business agility. He is a subject matter expert and senior advisor on topics related to scaling agility across an entire organization, allowing companies to realize the full benefits of Agile. At CA Technologies, Doug is the Senior Director of Agile Management and is an author, presenter, and thought leader at events worldwide.

Laureen Knudsen is an award-winning senior business leader with a career that spans information technology, financial systems, health care systems, and analytics. Laureen has been responsible for business transformations to agility in regulated environments at four companies. She specializes in streamlined, regulated, auditable, and Agile business processes for all methods of delivery and creating key indicators to ensure success. Laureen is passionate about mobilizing and educating executives to use best practices and continually improve, while ensuring they have the data they need to run their businesses.

About the Technical Reviewer

Rick Langsford is a Senior Advisor with the CA Technologies Transformation Program team. Rick's primary focus is empowering customers with insights into leveraging these new approaches to accelerate application and service delivery. Prior to CA, Rick was a portfolio advisor with VMware, working with VMware customers and product management to develop their Cloud and Virtualization Management strategy. Before VMware, Rick was an advisory consultant for EMC, building joint services and product solutions for private cloud operations. Prior to recent roles at VMware and EMC, Rick was cofounder and Vice President at Pepperweed Consulting, leading services, sales and R&D. Rick's team at Pepperweed launched several successful consumer software products and, as Hewlett-Packard (HP) Software's largest IT management and automation consulting partner, Rick's consulting team delivered strategy, process, and implementation consulting for many of HP's largest and most complex enterprise engagements. Rick holds a BS in Computer Technology from Purdue University and currently resides with his family in sunny Tampa, Florida.

Acknowledgments

The ideas in this book are the result of many conversations with and learning from many clients and colleagues. I have long been a consultant or speaker but find that I, more often than not, learn far more than those I am helping or speaking to. Thank you to everyone who has suffered through me at the whiteboard "explaining" a new idea I have for how to make this Agile thing work better. Laureen Knudsen, my partner in writing this book, is one of the Agile thought leaders at CA Technologies, so Laureen not only has to put up with me at work, but also in working to write together. I would like to especially thank Laureen for her ideas, knowledge, and the hard work she put into making this book a reality.

I would be remiss if I didn't thank some of the other members of CA:

Rick Langsford

Dan Rice

Brett Mullins

Ian McGinnis

Christopher Pola

Emily McRae

Marla Schimke

Noel Rodriguez

And a special thanks to:

Matt Strazza

Chris Schwartz

Chris and Matt make up the best management team that I've had the pleasure of working for.

Laureen and I work with these amazing people on a daily basis and we drew many of our examples of what is it to be truly agile from them. Thanks very much to each of you.

I have enjoyed writing this very much—it is my fondest wish that it will be helpful and that people will enjoy reading it.

—Doug Dockery

Along with those mentioned above, I'd like to thank Doug for taking this journey with me, and Kurt Hopke and Denise Hart-Pesek for the support, guidance, and inspiration they have provided me for the past 20 years.

—Laureen Knudsen

Introduction

"What important truth do very few people agree with you on?" Think about that question for a moment. You might find, as we did, that it is very difficult to give an intellectually honest answer. We wish we could take credit for coming up with this remarkable question, but it comes from Peter Thiel's amazing book, *Zero to One*.[1]

Perhaps an easier way to frame your answer is in this format:

Many people believe in x; but the truth is actually the opposite of x.

In the time since reading Thiel's book, we have thought of many answers:

- Many executives believe that there is no way to tell where all of their development dollars are being spent, but if you are doing disciplined Agile development, every dollar is accounted for.

- Many people who run product development companies believe that strategic planning pays off, yet very few can show how the products being developed align to those strategies.

Unfortunately, almost everything we came up with was simply taking a side in an existing argument about politics, global conflict, religion, and so on. What led us to write this book was the following answer to Thiel's question: Many people and businesses believe that "doing Agile" will solve all their business and organizational problems; but the truth is that "doing Agile," especially team-level agility, isn't the same as being an Agile organization. And, quite frankly, "doing Agile" is not of very much real value.

It might seem strange that the "Agile folks" who have worked for some of the truly Agile companies in the United States would say that "doing Agile" does not provide much real value. All too often, though, we see many companies who are "doing Agile" that simply adopt a series of processes or esoteric ceremonies. Unfortunately, often they find this exercise to be largely useless.

---

[1] Peter Thiel, *Zero to One* (New York: Crown Business, 2014).

Others believe that their organization should be "doing Agile" but think that agility is something that is wholly in the domain of the more technical members of their team—it's an information technology (IT) thing, so the human resources (or finance, marketing, or sales) department wouldn't benefit from it. Neither idea could be further from the truth. It is our hope that, by the end of this book, you will agree that the idea of process adoption of any kind should be met with a resounding "So what?" and agree that the true goal of agility is to maximize the creation of value across all parts of your organization.

So, if value is the goal of agility, what does value mean? For the purposes of this book, value is defined as making or saving money for yourself or your company. We believe that prioritization by value—that is, the determination of what work makes or saves the most money at this specific moment in time—is the foundational principle of the adoption of agility, not process or abstract ceremony. Simply put, value is creating the right thing at the right time.

We are often bombarded with the idea that it doesn't matter what you do as long as you do it well. This is, of course, completely untrue. It does matter what you do, because what you do should create value. The process of being an Agile organization requires the expenditure of capital and a great deal of effort. Doing so without creating value for the future is to miss the forest for the sake of a single process tree.

Before we get too far ahead of ourselves, though, let's explore what Agile is, what it means, and where it came from, and why you, as an executive, can benefit.

Agile?

What Does Agile Have to Do with running a Business?

So what's this Agile thing we keep talking about?

Agile is a mindset and a way of working together to get things done. It officially started in 2001 when the Manifesto for Agile Software Development[1] was penned. It consists of a set of principles that define best practices for taking an idea and creating a product. These principles cover creating the right level of plans at the right time, ensuring quality is part of every step in the process, and admitting that change is a part of everything we do, so plan for change. Originally, Agile practices were specifically designed for software development, but they have since been scaled to all areas of a company.

Agile Manifesto? The Unabomber had a manifesto. You might be thinking that you don't want to be part of anything that has a manifesto, but stick with us for a moment.

Agile, in its simplest form, is simply common sense. We have had customers tell us, on a fairly regular basis, that they didn't want to "do Agile." They seemed shocked when we told them we didn't want them to "do Agile" either. Instead, can we agree that you would be okay with doing these things?

---

[1]See http://agilemanifesto.org/

© CA 2018
D. Dockery and L. Knudsen, *Modern Business Management*,
https://doi.org/10.1007/978-1-4842-3261-3_1

- Working in small batch sizes

- Getting done with things before you start something else

- Proving that you are done and that you have created what your team committed to create

- Taking responsibility and accountability for what you commit to doing

- Working together and harnessing the power of your organization vs. that of a single team or individual

- Constantly learning

Nobody has ever told us no. That's Agile, though. It's not some crazy, new-age process that involves granola and yoga. It means working in the simplest way possible and focusing on the value that we are creating.

If you remember, we defined value as making or saving money for yourself or your company. Agile, therefore, is simply removing everything that gets in the way of creating value and allowing teams of people to determine best how that value should be created.

Simple, right? It's the simplest thing you will ever try to do, but at the same time, it is one of the hardest things there is to do well.

Agile Manifesto

In February 2001, 17 software developers met at the Snowbird resort in Utah to discuss lightweight development methods. They published the Manifesto for Agile Software Development, which you have most likely heard of by now. The manifesto is often written to be four bullet points, with a very important sentence to start the manifesto.

MANIFESTO FOR AGILE SOFTWARE DEVELOPMENT

We are uncovering better ways of developing software by doing it and helping others do it. Through this work we have come to value:

- Individuals and interactions over processes and tools

- Working software over comprehensive documentation

- Customer collaboration over contract negotiation

- Responding to change over following a plan

That is, while there is value in the items on the right, we value the items on the left more.

Kent Beck	James Grenning	Robert C. Martin
Mike Beedle	Jim Highsmith	Steve Mellor
Arie van Bennekum	Andrew Hunt	Ken Schwaber
Alistair Cockburn	Ron Jeffries	Jeff Sutherland
Ward Cunningham	Jon Kern	Dave Thomas
Martin Fowler	Brian Marick	

© 2001, the above authors

this declaration may be freely copied in any form, but only in its entirety through this notice.

When we were originally taught the manifesto, way back when Agile was new, it was the first sentence that was the meat of it: We are constantly striving for better ways of doing things (in the original case, developing software) by doing it and helping others to do it. This is the heart of agility, and it works as we bring Agile principles and practices into every area of our businesses and our lives.

Regarding the bullet points on the manifesto, although the secondary concerns were important, the primary concerns were more critical to success.

Please note that the manifesto says "over." Many people misrepresent the value statements. People will say things like "Agile doesn't do documentation," or "Agile doesn't plan." Obviously both of these statements are untrue. The manifesto says that documentation is important, but working software is more important. The same is true for each line above: The second item is important, but the first one is critical.

What did the manifesto writers mean by these terms?

- *Individuals and interactions*: Self-organization and motivation are important, as are interactions like colocation and pair programming. The ceremonies in Agile practices are important because they bring people together and make them have discussions and gain agreements based on consensus. Stories were originally known as "placeholders for a conversation." To best communicate ideas and requirements, conversations are far superior to written documents. That doesn't mean we don't take notes on what we agree to or include acceptance criteria so we know when something is done, but the conversation is never skipped in favor of a longer written document.

- *Working software:* Working software is more useful and welcome than just presenting documents to clients or executives in meetings. In Agile practices, we have a "definition of done" so that when someone talks about working software, they mean it meets a certain level of completion, often including being fully tested, the application programming interface (API) is working, and it's in a ready-to-consume state. Therefore, "working software" or completed work of any kind is much more beneficial to a company than a detailed written plan. This doesn't mean we don't plan—we do planning at the right time and increase the details of the plan each time we do it. Something will have high-level plans at first, but as it is ready to be pulled into an iteration or sprint it will be broken down and details will be fleshed out.

- *Customer collaboration*: How many times have you created exactly what someone originally asked for, only to be told that wasn't what they really wanted? Agile works to deal with these types of recurring issues. It is assumed that requirements cannot be fully collected at the beginning of the software development cycle, therefore continuous customer or stakeholder involvement is very important. Plans will be updated. Designs will change as we see the results of the initial work. If you do custom work, the contracts with your customers must allow for this, especially if you are using iterative wireframing, iterative prototyping, or other current methods of design. The way we do business is changing to acknowledge and allow for these changes to initial requirements and designs—even contracted and custom work.

- *Responding to change*: Agile methods are focused on quick responses to change and continuous development. Because we know plans always change, we plan for these changes. No longer do we require heavy change control processes. We acknowledge that every plan will change, so we can develop "good enough" plans and start working them, knowing we can modify them as we go along. There are very few instances where this cannot happen today— and many of these instances are due to regulations.

Use logic when deciding the level of commitment to these practices for your organization. Be part of the discussion and don't allow your execution teams to convince you that the things on the right in the bullets are not important or required in Agile practices.

Agile Principles

The Agile Manifesto is based on 12 principles,[2] and although these principles were originally written specifically for software development, we discuss them in a manner to show you how they can apply to any work.

1. *"Our highest priority is to satisfy the customer through early and continuous delivery of valuable software."* Deliver as frequently as your market will allow. If you are still delivering your products on-premises, your release cycles might be longer, but include your customers in design reviews, beta programs, and reviewing along the way. Work to modularize your systems so they can be delivered in smaller increments. How you design your product will play an important role in how satisfied your customers are and in how quickly you can gain some value.

   The pictures in Figure 1-1 show why it is important to include your customers in your designs and why it's important to have the right design as you progress toward your goals.

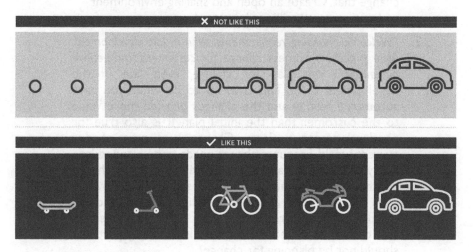

Figure 1-1. The importance of customer input and good design

---

[2]See http://agilemanifesto.org/principles.html

How do you think the customer would react to a design showing the first line of drawings? They gain no real value until the fifth version. Would that work for products you buy? Then why do you accept that for any work done in your organization? The second line of drawings shows how we can release each piece as a product and the customer will gain some benefit from it. They won't get everything they requested until the fifth release, just as in the first line of drawings, but they will gain some value.

For some percentage of customers, the products you design along the second line will be exactly what they want. Some people only have bicycles. Some have motorcycles and that is sufficient. Many people want and need a car, but giving them the products along the way allows them to experience the direction in which you are heading and make requests for changes or enhancements along the way. This isn't just for creating products, though. Everything you do should be reviewed early. If there is any part of your organization that is not showing their work early and often, change that. Create an open and sharing environment and save yourself millions in wasted work.

2. *"Welcome changing requirements, even in late development. Agile processes harness change for customer's competitive advantage."* We plan for change, even late in the development cycle. This is easier to do when you have automated testing and the changes provide more value to the customer than the initial plan. It is also true for nondevelopment projects. Change is a part of our current world. Frequent change needs to be planned into every process you have. If you are still using heavy change control management or find yourself locking down a plan, stop and think about how realistic it is to be doing that today. Do you really have any part of your business that can afford to be locked down? Is there any part that should not be planning for change?

What if you could harness that change to provide a competitive advantage? We worked with one company that became fully agile. They were not only able to respond to customer requests late in the development cycle, but they were able to see the value of each item of work being done. The chief technology officer (CTO) came up with an idea for a product that added a level of cybersecurity for anyone who used it. They were able to stop less valuable work, and flow the new work to the available teams. This not only allowed them to provide great benefit to their customers, but it added millions in revenue to their own bottom line.

We'll talk more about changing plans later. Just remember that Agile practices are based on logical thought and don't require you to do things that make no sense.

3. *"Deliver working software frequently, from a couple of weeks to a couple of months, with a preference to the shorter timeline."* Refer back to Figure 1-1 for insight. The more frequently we can deliver a product, the more value we can provide to the customer and the easier it is for us to get it right (to gain feedback so we can provide exactly what the customers want). Delivering more frequently allows us to ensure we are providing products that customers value and the feedback we receive from the released products helps us make sure all enhancements we plan are the ones requested most by our users.

   This is not just about product development, though. Sharing frequently is key. It's not that we are making products so much more quickly or doing work much more quickly, it's that we are showing people a less finished product than we used to, which also diminished the cost of failure. It's easier to redesign part of the scooter shown in Figure 1-1 than it would be to redesign the car. Early and frequent feedback saves you money and it saves you from creating something that no one wants to use.

   Many years ago, it was common to not demo or show your work until you considered it fully complete. This is no longer acceptable, nor can you keep up with the market this way. We now find companies using this technique in their marketing departments with campaigns, sales departments with opportunities, and human resources (HR) departments with new training and compensation plans. How we do business is changing, and Agile techniques are being used in all areas of the business.

4. *"Business people and developers must work together daily throughout the project."* Close, daily cooperation between business people and developers—this should really say both sides of every project, because these principles apply to any project type, not just software development and information technology (IT)—is critical. Every project has a customer and a team that completes the work. The stakeholders must be involved consistently to get the right outcome delivered as quickly as possible.

For software development and IT, the business knows strategy, the markets, and keeps abreast of current trends. The developers (and quality assurance [QA] folks) know how to build great products and they keep abreast of the latest technological breakthroughs. Creating a trusted relationship and team that includes both the business and technical sides of your products is mandatory to doing good Agile practices. They need each other and each other's knowledge to create the best product in your market.

Look at every part of your organization and make sure they aren't doing work in a vacuum or in a silo.

5. *"Build projects around motivated individuals. Give them the environment and support they need, and trust them to get the job done."* Trust that your teams know what they are doing. If the teams, or your business leaders, or your employees cannot be trusted you have a huge problem, one that cannot be cured by micromanaging or process. One of the best outcomes that we have seen come out of well-followed Agile practices is an increase in employee morale. This comes from people feeling they have ownership in their product and the work that they do. It also brings a respect and understanding of the other people that they might work with and depend on.

   Trust those you hire to do their jobs and to do them well. Provide coaching and advice and have discussions so the outcomes are known by all involved. It is really amazing what happens to a corporate culture when employees are trusted and the assumption is made that everyone wants to do a good job. If something goes wrong, maybe someone needs coaching on how to do that task better, but you believe that they want to do their best. Motivate your teams by trusting that they know what they are doing and that they will do the right thing for the company.

6. *"The most efficient and effective way of conveying information to and within a development team is face-to-face conversation."* Discussions, arguments, trade-off decisions, explanations, agreements: All of these types of conversations are needed as a product is being developed. You cannot do these things effectively through e-mail, written documents, or chat programs. Talk to each other. If everyone cannot be colocated, make sure full teams are as colocated as they can be. We dig into this more later in the book.

7. *"Working software is the principal measure of progress."* What if your status reports were based on working software that met an agreed-on definition of done, across all of your development teams? So, when someone said a certain feature was 50% complete, that means that it is really 50% complete and that half of that product not only works but doesn't need to be touched again—it is ready to ship. This is quite a difference from the verbal updates given at weekly or biweekly status meetings, where you never know how much technical debt or defect work you are collecting. With good Agile practices, you should have almost daily updates to the status of the work being done against your strategy for every project in your organization without needing to interrupt the teams to ask. These are the data you need to run your business in today's market. We dive deeper into this concept later.

   Every piece of work that is done in your organization, not just development projects, should align to a standard definition of done. These definitions will be different depending on the type of work being done, but you should have standards in your organization all the same. Agile does not mean throwing out policies and standards. It actually encourages definitions for quality of work so that everyone knows and is allowed to meet expectations. Set your people up to succeed by sharing expectations of "done" for every project in your organization.

8. *"Agile processes promote sustainable development. The sponsors, developers and users should be able to maintain a constant pace indefinitely."* This is known as *sustainable pace* and it is another mandatory concept in Agile. We've all read the articles about how work–life balance is important. Sustainable pace equates to the capacity of your teams. It's the rate of work they can agree to complete where they have to remain focused and driven each week, but they get to go home at a reasonable hour and not come in on weekends. It's the rate at which they can work, week after week, and not burn out. Every part of your organization should have a defined sustainable pace and working outside of that pace should be a rare occurrence, not the norm.

Nor should working beyond a sustainable pace be rewarded. We can't tell you how many times we have seen people work themselves into sickness or even the need to be hospitalized. These people are then praised by their organizations for their heroics. This incentivizes the wrong behavior. How much more work could that person have gotten done and at an improved quality by working at a pace that allowed them to stay healthy? Make sure you are requiring your teams at all levels to work at a sustainable pace.

9. *"Continuous attention to technical excellence and good design enhances agility."* What more can be said here? Let the technical people create good technical design, within reason. By within reason we mean within the guidelines of your open source policies, the riskiness of using a new technology, and other practices that are generally part of your development standards. This one principle can be a defining factor as to why a good developer will choose your organization over another. Being known for having technical excellence, both within your organization and in the products you sell, enhances your status as a business. The best designers, developers, and engineers generally will go where the best design, development, and engineering are being done.

   This principle holds true for other areas as well. There should always be attention to excellence and good work in every area of your organization. If any areas of your company are not continuously improving, you are falling behind your competition.

10. *"Simplicity—the art of maximizing the amount of work not done—is essential."* We talk to many people who really don't understand this concept. It seems simple at first, but it takes a good understanding of a process or flow to be able to successfully eliminate all waste from it. Stop doing things because some industry-standard process or consultant said you should, and do the things that make logical sense for your organization. If every single person in your company looked at the work he or she did on a daily basis and kept doing only those things that were really necessary, you could raise your productivity greatly and dramatically reduce wasted effort.

    Maximize the amount of work not done. In everything you do, ask yourself if it is important and necessary.

11. *"Best architectures, requirements, and designs emerge from self-organizing teams."* Every level of your organization needs to be able to make decisions. Be sure you aren't including unnecessary levels of management into decisions when they could be made by empowered teams. Again, when setting your processes and practices within your organization, use logic and remove ego. Push responsibility down into your organization and spread it out to all. Trust your employees to do the jobs they are hired to do. You can verify without micromanaging.

    Self-organizing does not mean that everyone gets to decide who they work with, what they do, and how they do it. For companies to be successful, you need practices and principles to which everyone adheres. We hear many times that executives are told that Agile means teams get to pretty much do whatever they want. This is patently untrue, as you can see by this list of principles.

12. *"At regular intervals, the team reflects on how to become more effective, then tunes and adjusts its behavior accordingly."* Everyone in your organization should regularly retrospect on what they do and how they do it. Even you. Every team should be looking to improve how they work. What does this mean? Each time a project, decision, or proposal is complete, the people involved review how it went, what they want to continue doing, what they would like to stop doing, what should change, and what should stay the same. Choosing just the top one or two things that people want to change and making those changes a reality can cause a large increase in productivity and reduction in issues. Continuously solving for the top one or two things that cause pain can help an organization thrive.

    We're frequently asked what a company should tackle first or what they should do next. We tell them to look at the things causing them the most pain. Solve for those things, then find the biggest pains and do it again. A pain can be a productivity inhibitor, a cause of frustration, or something that negatively affects morale. Find the things causing your organization the most pain and use Agile principles to solve for that problem.

    This is vital in today's fast-paced and changing world. Continuous improvement is key to your organization's success.

Agile Methods Used Today

Agile started with development teams and often covered how to technically design, develop, and test a product. As time has gone on, Agile practices and principles are being applied to every area of the business.

There are many flavors of Agile and you can find definitions of them easily by searching the Internet. We describe why the methods are important to leaders and executives and what you should know about them. Here are the most commonly used flavors of Agile.

Scrum

Scrum is the most widely used flavor of Agile and the one that has been scaled by many different organizations. It started with development teams but most of its principles can be used for any type of project. It is represented by short time periods of work (called time boxes) with a specific definition of done. It features static teams that don't change iteration to iteration or release over release. Work flows to the teams rather than having a team formed around a project. It is a disciplined approach to development and requires the team to be self-leading and to take responsibility for meeting their commitments to the company and for the outcome they produce (see Figure 1-2). It also requires a team to improve themselves and their processes continuously.

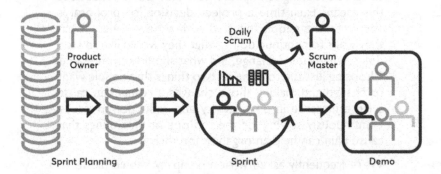

Figure 1-2. Scrum basics

Done correctly, it works very well in almost any environment and with every team in your organization. The basics of scrum principles and the goals that are attained can benefit every part of your company. Having a stack-ranked backlog, small batch sizes, and short time boxes where people demonstrate what they got done at the end can reduce risk in any type of work. Continuously looking at how you work, what the issues are, and how to resolve them is a best practice for everyone.

Kanban

Kanban is a method for managing work that balances demands for work with the available capacity for new work. Work items are visualized to give participants a view of progress and process, from task definition to customer delivery. Team members "pull" work as capacity permits, rather than work being "pushed" into the process when requested.

Kanban provides a visual process-management system that aids decision making about what, when, and how much to produce. The method was inspired by the Toyota Production System and lean manufacturing, but it can be applied to any project or professional service and is especially beneficial for teams that don't have planned work. Examples include teams that fix bugs as they are called in from customers or IT operations teams that process requests for new servers. There aren't batches of work to plan into iterations, and flowing the work through the team, when it is imperative it be done as quickly as possible, is key.

If your teams have batched work including releases of more than a few days, enhancements that take more than one user story, and on-premises releases, and they want to use Kanban, be sure cycle time is one of your metrics (the time it takes for each item of work to be complete). In our experience, even very disciplined Agile teams seem to slow down if they use Kanban and don't give themselves time boxes.

Kanban is also being used by many companies to manage the program-level work and strategy-level work. Leadership teams create a flow based on the steps needed to put a new idea into their strategy backlog, or flesh out the idea into work that can be given to the execution teams.

Extreme Programming

Extreme Programming (XP) was quite popular with software engineers when Agile was new. XP touts that it takes best practices to extreme levels. Key tenets of XP are paired programming, short releases with frequent checkpoints, extensive code reviews, and unit testing (see Figure 1-3). It has been used successfully in many companies but generally focuses on development teams. One facet of XP, paired programming, works well in some environments and generally doesn't work in others. From our experience, pairing works best with more extroverted developers rather than introverted developers.

Planning/Feedback Loops

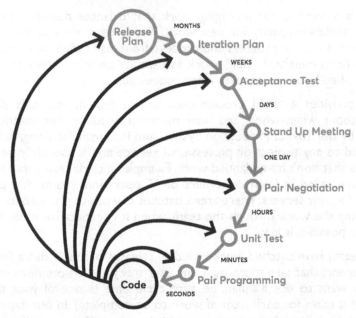

Figure 1-3. Extreme Progrmming

Lean

Lean principles have become the basis for many of the other Agile practices. The core of Lean is to maximize value while minimizing waste. There are sayings in other Agile practices that mean the same thing: maximizing the amount of work not done, for example.

Lean thinking changes the focus of management from optimizing specific technologies, resources, and groups to optimizing the flow of products and services through entire value streams that flow horizontally across the organization.

Lean usually focuses on three main areas:

- *Purpose*: Essentially this is focusing on creating value for others to bring value to ourselves. Solving customers' problems so they will find value in your solutions, and pay you for them, is creating value for you.

- *Process*: Reviewing every process, from start to finish, and optimizing the whole. Optimizing one portion of a process wreaks havoc in other areas and causes bottlenecks.

- *People*: Making sure every process has someone who ensures it is as efficient and effective as possible. Not one person per department or organization, but one person per process, end to end. This person continually ensures you are improving how you work.

You can, and should, apply Lean principles to every area of your business.

Lean Startup

Lean Startup is based on a book by the same name written by Eric Ries.[3] It was originally written to provide a scientific approach to creating and managing startups and to get a product into customers' hands faster. However, many large corporations have started to use the main principles for innovative projects. It gives real-world steps to remove waste from your design and development processes and ways to ensure you create a product in which customers will find value.

Design Thinking

Design thinking is a method for practical and creative resolution to market problems and the creation of solutions. It is a form of solution-based, or solution-focused thinking with the intent of producing a valuable, future result. By considering both present and future conditions, several alternative solutions may be explored.

Isn't Agile Just for IT or Software Development?

The short answer is "No, it's not." As an executive, if you are thinking this way, you are missing out on a great opportunity for yourself and your organization.

Agile practices can be used any time you need to plan something, create something, work with others, communicate, increase productivity, become more predictable, or eliminate waste from your business. If you are sticking to the Agile principles, you can apply them to almost any part of your life.

We know people who have daily standups with their children each morning. It's a great way to know what is going on in everyone's lives in a very short amount of time. We know families that have Kanban boards hanging in their homes for chores, home-improvement projects, and other things they need to do.

---

[3]Eric Ries, *Lean Start-up* (New York: Crown Business, 2011).

You can use Lean and Agile principles and practices in every part of your business. To be honest, if you aren't looking at removing waste from every process within your organization, if you aren't looking at communicating verbally instead of sending e-mails or giving out documents to read, you are falling behind your competition.

Still holding a biweekly status meeting? Stop. There are more effective and efficient ways to work with your teams. Every part of our organizations need to implement Agile principles and practices.

Begin to push knowledge and control down in the organizational structure. Share how the company is doing with everyone. Give responsibility, and therefore ownership, to everyone. We routinely ask engineers if they would be proud to put a plaque on their product with their names on it, or have a banner with their names in the software they create. We can't tell you how many say "No." If the people creating the products don't take enough responsibility for them that they would be proud to put their name on them, then you have a problem (and your customers are not receiving value).

We constantly hear executives say they can't do these things, that these ideas and concepts won't work at their companies, or that they are so far removed from this desired state that they can't get there. Then we work with companies who are willing to try, who are succeeding at doing business in a new way, And who are sharing the burdens and rewards with their employees. It not only works, but those companies are pulling ahead of their competition.

Quite frankly, if you aren't willing to change the way you do business, you probably won't have a business to change for very long.

But I'm an Executive; What's in It for Me?

Agile practices might be one of the greatest benefits to executives that we have seen in our decades of work. So many have no idea, though, and are spending millions of dollars on a transformation that has no benefit to their organization.

What if we told you that when using good disciplined Agile practices, you should know where every dollar of your development and IT spend is going? What if you could not only know where every dollar is spent but be able to see how you can use your teams more effectively to respond to market changes? What if you could see, day to day, how your teams are creating value and that all work aligns to your strategies?

We describe how in the remainder of this book.

My Contrarian View

Or All Unhappy Companies Are Different

At the beginning of *Anna Karenina,* Tolstoy states, "Happy families are all alike; every unhappy family is unhappy in its own way." Likewise, all successful Agile adoptions are the same—they focus on the creation of value and bringing people together; but each unhappy Agile adoption is unhappy in its own way.

In a book about Agile/Lean adoption and the benefits of becoming a Lean/Agile organization, it might seem counterproductive to talk about why organizational change fails. However, we feel that we learn much more from failure than from success.

One of my favorite sports personalities is Bill Belichick, who at the time of this writing is the coach of the New England Patriots. Belichick famously talks about not remembering wins or positive plays, instead focusing on negative outcomes in his never-ending cycle of attempting to improve. Belichick has had a Hall of Fame career, but immediately at the end of each game he focuses on the things his team could have done better vs. the things they did well. Although his approach might seem extreme to some, it certainly illustrates how many extraordinary people learn from what is deemed by others as "failure."

© CA 2018
D. Dockery and L. Knudsen, *Modern Business Management,*
https://doi.org/10.1007/978-1-4842-3261-3_2

With that in mind, the following sections describe the primary failure modes of business transformation.

Lack of Executive Leadership

There must be leadership who understand, at least at a high level, the outcomes that need to be achieved and earmarks of good adoption for a business transformation to succeed. It doesn't matter where you are transitioning from or what you are transitioning to. Leaders must stand behind the changes that occur and provide leadership to get there. You cannot tell your teams to "do as I say, not as I do" because they will try to get around the directive at every turn.

Training the execution or development teams and not the leadership can cause many issues within an organization. Teams can define "Agile" in any way they want if the leaders cannot say differently. When a leader becomes involved in a project, usually because the wheels have fallen off, the leader can single-handedly derail an entire transformation in one day by asking for metrics that don't exist in Agile environments. We have seen leaders demand teams start using traditional methods and blame agility for slowing down a project, when in actuality it's just the first time the leader has seen the true capacity of the team.

Agile methods will highlight every issue a team is having. Suddenly, a leader can see every process misstep, every communication issue, and every poor estimation that their teams make. We have seen leaders panic as Agile methods start to make every issue a team is having transparent to everyone in the organization. We have seen the leaders blame Agile methods themselves and say they don't work, because it was more comfortable to sit in a room and agree that a team was 95% sure they could complete a project on time, on budget, in scope, and with the resources allocated, even when everyone knew those plans were untrue.

You cannot fix issues if you hide them or punish teams for having them. Expect that all of your issues will be highlighted as teams take on more and more Agile practices. Expect that this will happen at every level in the organization where you adopt Agile practices. Know that this will happen and lead your teams through it. When we used to lead Agile transformations for corporations, we used to tell executives that there was some information (metrics) they weren't allowed to see for a year. The data were for the team only. After a year of training, coaching, and mentoring, if the team was still struggling, then we might have a personnel issue and at that point they could have access to the data.

We also find that lack of executive leadership involvement means that the leaders cannot tell if they are transforming correctly or not. Teams get away with doing "Agile their way," which often leads to what we call *feral Agile teams*. These are teams that don't work together, don't adopt similar best practices, and don't produce any more data to steer your business than they did when using traditional practices. As a matter of fact, they often produce less because leadership cannot tell them why they are wrong when they say that Agile means no planning, no estimating, and no release dates.

Making sure your entire executive team learns enough about Agile and how to apply it to gain the most value for your organization is mandatory for organizational transformation. Ensuring the practices your teams adopt are consistent so you have the data you need to run your business is vital.

Lack of executive leadership drives all other failure modes. We generally see one of two scenarios in this situation:

- Skunk Works operation
- Checkbook commitments

Skunk Works

The designation *skunk works* originated in aerospace and is generally used in product development businesses to describe a team in their organization given a high degree of autonomy, and who don't have to follow the rules. When we first heard of skunk works, it related to teams who were working on cutting-edge, incubator, or secret projects. In some companies, every Agile team becomes a skunk works team and no longer has to abide by any best practices, processes, or oversight. This is not Agile.

A few years back, and in some areas of the world where agility is just starting to catch on, we see the Agile transformation being done as a skunk works project. The teams start using Agile practices without approval. They hide their new skills from management for fear of being shut down. They try to bypass or evade product life cycle processes, including gates, milestones, and oversight.

Having an Agile organization will only benefit you as an executive. If you find this is happening in your organization, go talk to the teams and give them the support they need to be successful. Let them become the pilot program and leaders of your Agile transformation. If you have many teams who are all applying Agile practices differently, have them determine a consistent, agreed-on way of applying the principles so you can have consistency. It will greatly benefit your organization in the long run.

Checkbook Commitments

We see this so frequently in companies that it's becoming commonplace. An executive decrees the change to Agile delivery across the entire IT or product development organization. Lately they are decreeing they are to become an Agile business! However, there's no real follow-through, knowledge of the goals they are trying to reach, reason they are moving in this direction, or knowledge of how the executives themselves will need to change their behavior: It's simply a "checkbook commitment." More often than not these days, it's a commitment of pennies and not even a check to get the help the teams need to be successful.

The executive demands results, yet doesn't change the metrics by which success is measured. He or she also asks for things that don't exist in Agile practices, like Gantt charts. These leaders continue to hold weekly or biweekly staff meetings and show that they are not committed to changing their own actions to support an Agile business. They keep people in place to "drive" the projects to completion.

Unengaged, the executive proclamation for an Agile adoption will never move to a true business transformation, no matter how much money you spend.

Think about that for a minute. At best, without the executive's continued engagement, the organization will only have pockets of Agile success, typically limited to the team level. The business will never see an increase in quality or productivity, get products to market more quickly, or respond to the market any better than they did before they "went agile."

Teams will move away from the light discipline they had under waterfall processes to a more chaotic coding method with no planning, no idea of when something will be done, and no data to give a good project status. Leadership will lose sight of what they are getting for the millions being spent in their organization. The organization will likely grow to blame Agile (and each other) for decreased quality, productivity, and insight into the value being created.

The executive's resignation letter will conveniently not include the word "Agile" in its summary of successes.

Failure to Transform Leader Behavior

We cannot even begin to count the number of people in leadership roles who we talk to who believe that an Agile transformation will not affect them or their own behaviors. Transformation is a journey that includes every person in an organization.

Leadership must make a personal commitment to each other and their teams, and expect a commitment from their teams to truly transform a business.

You need to commit to your peers that you will stop running your business with false data and assumptions. Here is an example of what we mean: At the start of both of our careers we were part of product teams that planned using waterfall or iterative and incremental approaches that were governed by a phase-gate process. To clear Phase 2, we presented plans and hundreds of pages of documents that proved we could meet a certain date, with a specific scope, budget, team, and quality level. Everyone sitting in that room knew that this would never happen. Everyone knew we weren't 95% sure we could meet this plan. Everyone agreed we could meet the plan and congratulated us for creating a plan to get the work done. We see this type of thing happen all the time and it has become a standard way of running a business. We see it in strategy meetings where the market analysis numbers are made up or not current, we see it in planning meetings for projects on which we are basing our revenue projections, we see it in sales planning meetings, and so on. It seems somewhere along the line we went from running our businesses on real data to pretending that the made-up numbers were valid.

If you are in a business that does this, stop now. Start calling each other on it and agree that the decisions made based on the false data are probably not the right decisions. If this is all the data you have right now to use in making decisions, then do the best you can, but stop pretending that those plans won't change. Promise yourself and your teams that starting today you will all be allowed to voice when something isn't real. You will make the best decisions you can while you work to get real data, and you must agree that the plans made will change.

So what commitments do you need to make to your teams? You need to commit to measure them differently. You'll start to measure value delivery over meeting a schedule, that working software will be valued over software specifications. You also need to promise them that you will provide them with the training they need not only to learn the basics of an Agile method, but also to engage in continuous learning. You will need to understand the methods well enough so you can back them up when someone questions them or when another leader asks for traditional project details. You must also promise that you will call them out when they want to revert back or not be transparent. You'll provide the guidance they need as they learn to work in a new way, especially at the beginning, when Agile practices are highlighting everything that is not being done correctly or that is going wrong.

Also promise them that you'll reward learning and celebrate even the small successes, that you understand the chaos curve of organizational change and will lead them through it, and that you will help them become predictable.

Leaders must accept that a successful transformation is a journey and seek guidance for a transformation with a broad, sustainable impact. Leaders make a personal commitment to their teams, and in turn they recognize the personal commitment they are asking of their teams.

In some of the most successful companies we've worked with, we find leaders who just get things done. They know the right actions to achieve success. They direct their teams to perform those actions, and they have the power to control all aspects of the work and do whatever it takes to get it done.

How often does that really happen?

Many times, in the not-so-successful companies, we find leaders telling the teams what to do, which generates a false sense of success via control. When a well-meaning leader powers through difficult circumstances regardless of the impact on the team, they leave the wisdom and the morale of the team behind. These types of leaders also reward heroics; those who work nights and weekends to get a job done, or those who are constantly jumping in to "put out fires." Quite frankly, if an organization is continually on fire and needs a hero to get the work done, it's not being run well. Planning is not done well or people would not need to work late nights and weekends on a regular basis. Unexpected events should not be the norm. Although these things occur in even the best run organizations, it's the frequency with which they occur that should sound the alarms. If your teams are constantly having to perform heroics to get their work done, take a step back and figure out how to get them to a sustainable pace. Often you need to slow down initially to move faster in the long run.

As leaders, we don't want to be standing behind our teams' back pushing buttons or pulling strings. Who has the time or desire to do that? Instead the leader needs to take a service-lead approach and use the following principles:

- *Systematic neglect:* In 1970, in his booklet titled *The Servant as Leader,* Robert K. Greenleaf identified two extreme types of leaders: those who thrive leading under pressure and those who endure pressure to lead.[1] The manager knows the limits of how much focus can be allocated to issues, and learns what to focus on and what to let go of to support the team and achieve goals effectively.

- *Acceptance:* A leader knows when to let go and trust the instincts of the team, accepts the wisdom of the team, and is prepared to support it. You pay the people on your teams for a reason. Trust them to get their jobs done. Almost everyone we meet wants to do a good job. If your teams are not succeeding, find out the real force behind the failure. It is rarely a lazy or unwilling team.

---

[1] Robert K. Greenleaf, *The Servant as Leader* (Atlanta, GA: Robert K. Greenleaf Center for Servant Leadership, 1970).

- *Listening*: A manager facilitates useful and necessary communication, pays attention to what remains unspoken, and is motivated to actively hear what others are saying. How often do you actively hear what others are saying or trying to tell you? As leaders of corporations, we get so busy and need to focus on so many different areas that it can be difficult to stop and really listen to what we are being told.

- *Language*: Leaders speak effectively and nondestructively; they clearly and consistently articulate the vision and goals for the team. Leaders need to fully understand their strategy and initiatives and be able to efficiently and effectively communicate these ideas to the teams, as well as have an understanding of how the teams' work will help the company meet those goals.

- *Values*: The manager is responsible for building a personal sense of values that are clearly exhibited through consistent actions. He or she supports team behaviors that build this sense of values. What values does your company truly support? What do you incent with your bonus programs? Do they align with the values you state to the public? We have worked with many companies whose core values state that they value teamwork, yet they incent people to work against each other and only bonus the individual. Make sure your actions align with your values.

- *Tolerance of imperfection*: A leader modulates his or her own sense of perfection and offers to each team member an understanding of their strengths and challenges, and cares more about "How can I help the team grow?" Giving teams the time they need to change how they work and understanding the change curve and what the teams will go through is vital. Agile is simple but not easy. It highlights every issue going on and can be quite uncomfortable at the beginning, especially for introverts. Encouraging teams throughout this process and supporting them as they learn is something every great leader must do.

- *Goal setting*: A leader owns the vision. He or she doesn't advocate for a personal belief in what is right, but rather maintains the goal for a higher purpose, inviting others to align with the vision for the overall good. Everyone in the company should have similar goals that they are working toward. Sharing those goals and why they are important is key to successfully leading teams. We see many organizations where lofty goals are described in jargon and they mean nothing to the front-line teams. Be sure you are setting goals that people can get behind and make sure everyone understands how they will be measured. Make those measurements visible so everyone plays a part in owning the outcome.

- *Personal growth*: The manager recognizes the value of continually finding diverse disciplines that invite new ways of acting in service to the team, and models this growth behavior to inspire others. Modeling how to always improve is an important quality in a good leader. We see many organizations that require their teams to continuously improve, but they don't follow a similar model. Requiring continuous improvement of our own practices and procedures models the best example for the teams.

- Withdrawal: A leader knows when to step back and allow the team to figure out its course, rather than inflicting a personal sense of what is right for the team. He or she carefully decides what to bring forward and when. Knowing when to provide guidance and how to provide it is imperative. As long as the team is following the standard requirements needed for you to get consistent data to run the business, they should be able to use the practices that suit them best. We often give options to help the team solve their pains or to help the team continuously improve.

No Change to Organizational Structure

How your organization is aligned can play a large role in whether Agile principles are adopted long term. Most people think this means restructuring their development teams to create entire product increments, but it goes beyond this.

We often ask questions like these:

- What is your current organizational structure?

- How many layers of management exist around each Agile team?

- How is governance perceived?

- What walls are required to be broken down over and over again for value to flow through the organization?

- What else do you ask your teams to do? What do you decree from on high?

We say we're changing but are we really?

- We ask how they measure performance and find specific metrics for various departments.

Typical organizations have been set up for suboptimization of corporate goals. They pit department leaders against each other and give bonuses and awards based on one group winning over another. This goes against the basic Lean principles of optimizing the whole. If you are doing this, you are not encouraging your people to do better; you are instead incenting them to belittle others' work.

We consulted with one company that incented individuals. Most of their bonuses were paid on the work done in addition to their job description. This sounds like a good idea, but over time it meant that people focused on the other things and didn't do their day jobs—some weren't even rated at all on how well they did the job they had been hired to do. It also meant that what was most important to each person was that his or her own idea won, not the best idea for the company. These employees would hide and step on some really great ideas so that their idea won. They would move forward with some initiatives so that it was too late for the other ideas to take hold. They, the individual, would win at any cost, and the cost often was to the company as a whole.

We limit visibility of the organization's overall effectiveness and focus on our team's success at the expense of success for the organization. Often, traditional metrics create accidental adversaries and enable finger pointing. Let's look to reframe what we measure and how we measure our teams to ensure the company and the customers are benefiting.

What if instead we measure value delivery? Think of the results we could achieve if we change our focus from individual success, hero work, and pitting employees against each other, and instead focus everyone on creating value for our customers. We could work together to optimize for the whole system.

We need to make sure that everyone associated with the value delivery has visibility into the current state of the value stream, including its blocks and bottlenecks. Successful Agile transformations understand the goal as successful delivery of value to the customer and they coordinate as a whole to deliver that value.

Is your organization clinging to the notion of resource utilization? This involves believing that loading people to 100% capacity is the best way to get work done, and measuring people annually by how well they deliver in this fully loaded mode.

We recently were talking to a company that paid attention to every hour of every employee's time. If a project came in two hours under schedule, they assigned new work to those people that took two hours. What do you think happened? Do you think any future projects ever came in ahead of schedule? This is completely predictable behavior based on actions, but discussions about these types of actions were met with blank looks and a resistance to do anything differently. This company was losing productivity because of how they tracked and managed their employees' time. There are much better ways to increase productivity. The processes and policies they had in place to increase productivity had the exact opposite outcome.

To incent greater productivity, collaboration, and communication, you need to revisit how you appraise work. Instead of annually, by individual, 100% utilized, with MBOs set 12 months earlier, invite frequent feedback and focus more on team effectiveness and outcomes. Bias performance appraisal toward efficiency of value flow versus efficiency of workers. We are seeing many organizations that base MBOs on cross-organizational outcomes, which drives and incents collaboration between departments, teams, and business units. With the right automation, you no longer have to rely on manually generated Gantt charts to see how well a team is working. You can tell how value delivery is progressing early in development, in real time, to make trade-off decisions based on real data. We talk about this in more detail in a later chapter.

No Change to How You Work

You have invested heavily in predictive model delivery practices (a politically correct way to say waterfall)—and you know your projects will always be late and cost more than they are supposed to—but you're comfortable with the practices and know how to effectively manage late projects within your organization. Maybe you are like the financial institution we recently visited. You are one of the largest financial players in the world but the people doing the work on your projects do not provide statuses; the project managers simply report how they "feel" about the work being done without a need for pesky facts.

You really want to be able to say you are delivering in a modern way, however. It might make the new people you have hired more comfortable as they settle into your company. You are in luck: Heavy, prescriptive frameworks are the new waterfall. We see far too many companies decide to simply rename what they are doing and pretend to be "Agile." One hundred-forty person teams are now "Agile teams." Multiyear projects are now made up of 12-week "sprints."

Two-hour status meetings are now "daily standups," where they don't happen daily, no one actually stands up, and someone assigns the day's work to the team members. We're Agile damn it, because we say we are. Even though we reap no real benefits from agility, we need something big and extremely complicated so we can justify our bad practices. Enter scaling frameworks.

To be fair, we really do not think the scaling frameworks that have become behemoths purposely cause this problem. Most of these frameworks, in the beginning, were a great idea. We have really gone too far, though, and they have become very bloated. In an effort to be everything to everyone, the modern crop of frameworks that companies adopt in a quest for "agility" have become incredibly heavy, prescriptive, and governance driven. When you need a several-hundred-page book to understand a framework that is guiding your efforts to produce value, something is wrong.

If we compare and contrast the concept of Agile, of Scrum, and of scaled frameworks, there are many interesting take-aways. Here are the first that came to us:

- Scrum has three roles: Scrum master, product owner, and team (everyone else). Some of the scaling frameworks have those same three roles plus at least 17 more. Agility was all about making the teams self-organizing and self-reliant as much as possible. Having so many people and roles needed for oversight eliminates this benefit.

- Scrum is described completely in the Scrum Guide, created by its founders Ken Schwaber and Jeff Sutherland, in 17 pages, and that includes the cover sheet, table of contents, and so on. Some of the scaling modalities devote almost as many words to describing single constructs in its hierarchy. Are complete descriptions bad? Of course not. If something is so complex, though, that you have to take 17 pages to describe one of more than a hundred parts, we have lost the concept of simple.

- Agile is defined as a philosophy of values that makes getting work done in the best way possible. The original manifesto is only a few paragraphs long. There are at least four different versions of some of the scaling methods—we see customers struggle for weeks deciding which one they want to adopt. If picking the thing that is supposed to make it easy to get to where you want to go is that hard, maybe things have become too complex.

Agile development is meant to be something you are, something your organization becomes. It's a journey, not a multi-hundred-icon-driven map to a very specific destination in a one-size-fits-all model. The proponents of frameworks will tell you that delivering value is hard in a complex environment, and there are many people that need to be involved. That is all true, but there is no need to replace your huge and complex waterfall software development life cycle (SDLC) with a huge and complex new one. Set your developers free: Allow them to decide how best to deliver value. Adopt common-sense practices like letting teams plan, work, and deliver together rather than following a highly prescriptive model that tells them how to do everything. People are not icons on a map; they are the true value of your organization. Forcing them into yet another complex, prescriptive model is not progress. It's simply the new waterfall.

No Business View of the Value Stream

Value stream is a phrase that is being used by many people to mean many things. In Lean, we talk about value stream mapping, which is a technique used to document a process as it exists today, then analyze it, optimize it, and continuously improve it. Others have started using value stream to mean a line of business, or a product (something valuable) that is delivered to customers. Still others say it's a method used to define, construct, and deliver something of worth to a customer.

For the purposes of this book we will be using the Lean view of a value stream: a process your organization uses to get something of value done. This can be any process, not just those that create products. Almost every process touches more than one department or group within your company so we need to make sure we understand who is involved, who is responsible, and where the bottlenecks are.

Think of your most important process. It's generally either the process that you use to create products and services or the one that allows you to collect money for providing value.

- Who is involved?
- Who is responsible for the entire process? Is there one person responsible!
- How are you incenting those that are involved in managing the people who participate?
- Are you optimizing the entire process or just a piece of it, as an indirect result of the incentive?
- Do you know where the bottlenecks are?

- Have you worked to mitigate them without negatively affecting the remainder of the process?

- Is someone optimizing their part of the process without seeing how that affects the entire process?

We have seen so many companies where they allow teams to optimize a small portion of a vital corporate process to the detriment of the company—and get highly rewarded for doing so! You need to have a clear line of sight from beginning to end, from ideation to utilization.

Most executives at companies we work with generally understand the process used to get a product created from ideation to release. They hear people complain about portions of the process but they don't know how to optimize the process to gain optimal proficiencies.

Today we are all in the software business and it is vital that we don't have process for process's sake or we will never be able to gain optimal efficiencies. Today it's about IT and product and technology organizations providing more value through product development. We find most organizations embraced silos, to the degree that even as they were adopting Agile practices, they did so in "Agile silos." They optimized the engineering teams, without optimizing QA. They develop products more quickly but can't get to them to market more quickly. We see companies optimizing parts of the organization, but not the whole. It's great that your development or IT teams are creating product more quickly, but if your marketing teams can only plan campaigns around major releases, or your sales teams are used to selling the next big feature, the rest of your company can break down. Collaboration and aligning around value streams is key.

We all have one or more value streams or we wouldn't have a business or a job. The goal is to map your system at whatever level of detail best articulates your sense of handoffs and bottlenecks, taking regulatory requirements into consideration. Those handoffs and bottlenecks represent delays and waste. We talk about optimizing a value stream later in this book.

Servant leaders don't relinquish all control; rather, they recognize the value in releasing control when all concerned are better served. The level of control changes. You no longer need to manage teams day to day or ask for weekly status reports. With disciplined Agile practices, your teams provide you with data you need to run your business and to make the key decisions so you can beat out your competition. Realigning your organization to optimize your key processes will increase productivity, predictability, and quality, and mitigate bottlenecks and pain points. Maintain centralized control when you see that this is in the best service to your teams, but let go of the reigns and trust them to get the work done.

Failure to Decentralize Control

In a modern business, you don't give up all control, you give up the need to control everything. Ensuring that decisions are made by the most qualified level in your organization can speed the pace of work, allow work to flow continuously, and ensure the best decisions are made.

When we talk about business agility, I like thinking about the ability to pivot and change as conditions do, or the ability to take advantage of opportunities. However, we also need to be cognizant of where the pivots occur in the organization.

Businesses need to pivot to drive their markets. Some of these are big pivots and some are small pivots. The big pivots happen at the portfolio and strategic level. Big pivots are things like changing what you invest in, adding a new strategy, and reallocating funds or people to a different area. Small pivots are made at the program or release level. They include technical decisions, architectural trade-offs, and decisions about providing broad functionality or deep functionality to create the most value. Big and small pivots should inform and influence each other.

Principles of Product Development Flow

There is a time to trust your teams and a time to provide oversight and guidance. Here are two basic rules for when to hold the reigns and when to let them loose:

- *The Scale Rule*: Centralize control for problems that are infrequent, large, or that have significant economies of scale.

- *The Perishability Rule*: Decentralize control for problems and opportunities that age poorly.

It's pretty common for large enterprises these days to have a wide disbursement of teams across many time zones. Some companies even implement 80/20 rules that guide projects to employ 80% offshore teams with only 20% of teams located in the same building (or the same city). This trend seems to swing like a pendulum: The next decade we see 70% in one country and 30% offshore. We now realize that certain types of work are best done in certain areas of the world, as countries optimize for various business roles.

When you have such distributed teams, it's even easier to fail at your Agile transformation. We have seen companies do things that directly contribute to these failures, such as these:

- Set up a complex geographic maze based on the economics of resource utilization.

- Ensure a time zone difference between 7 and 11 hours.

- Rely heavily on e-mails and large documents (especially detailed product requirements documents and test plans) for your communication.

- Definitely don't invest in bringing people together to collaborate or train.

- Trade face-to-face for late-night or early-morning telephone calls.

Many companies trade face-to-face collaboration for the promise of lower costs. For this technique to be successful, it is even more important that you have the right processes and tools in place and that you trust your teams to do the right thing. You need to ensure consistent practices are in place, a good tool that can be accessed by every team, and consistent understanding of your rules of play. By *rules of play,* we mean that if your engineers are in one country and your QA team is in another, everyone understands that the entire team (engineers and QA) are responsible for the quality. Work cannot be thrown over the metaphorical wall. Monitor the value stream progress and the flow of work when full teams or portions of your teams are distributed.

Ensure working agreements and communication plans are fully implemented and that these agreements and plans work across cultures in your organization. By definition, distributing work to teams around the world requires you to understand each culture, how they work, and what motivates them. How much control do you need over these teams? It doesn't matter where your company originates or which teams are "offshore" for you. What matters is that you take every culture and work environment into consideration.

With your distributed teams, how fast do you get feedback? One of the big mistakes we have seen over and over with distributed teams is that they use the same process and feedback loops as they did when they had all work originating in one country. When deciding where to put work in your global business, do you calculate the cost of delay in your return on investment (ROI) equation? Do you have people who know how to and who can mitigate the challenges of distributed teams for the entire organization? What is your escalation path when the constraints become overwhelming?

To solve for these problems, do the following:

- Hire a coach that knows how to work with distributed teams. Ask potential coaches how they solved these problems before. We can't tell you how many times we have been asked if we work with distributed teams and after one shallow, overly simplistic answer, we are accepted as knowledgeable. Make sure your candidates can articulate how they have solved for cost of delay, communication, and culture issues. They should be able to tell you in detail how they have put in place processes and tools that work worldwide so they could see progress against goals.

- Train everyone on the same Agile practices. This might seem like a given, but when you aren't training even your local teams on disciplined Agile practices and when you can't articulate at a high level what those practices are, there is no way this will happen worldwide. You must have a common understanding of things like a definition of done for stories, iterations, features, and releases. You must have the same toolset used to manage your stories, defects, tasks, test cases, and test run results so you can have your data normalized and you can have consistent data to run the company.

- Invest in high-definition, large-screen video technology to bring everyone's voice into the same room. Make sure the team can see each other frequently.

- Have a facilitator in each location when teams plan their dependent delivery commitments. During your planning cycles, you need to have your execution teams behaving as full teams and not as "us and them." Having someone who can facilitate these sessions is imperative.

- Whether using audio only or adding video, use facilitation techniques that ensure all insights are welcome (small-group brainstorming, round-robin check-ins, frequent breaks). It is especially important that you take all cultures into consideration when determining the best facilitation techniques to use.

- Invest in technologies that support transparent workflow communication. Your communication and discussion flows should allow fluid communication and discussion. As we bring new graduates into our workforce, they are more experienced at having discussions through electronic channels. Find a tool that has the features you need and use it consistently.

- Maintain a regular cadence of visits across all geographies and all roles. This item goes beyond where we talked about having team members spend extended periods of time at the other locations. Managers and executives need to be engaged at every location as well. We often see roadshows where executives go and give speeches to each location, which isn't very effective in the long run. Spend time talking to the team members, solving their issues, removing impediments for them, and really hearing from them what is working and what isn't.

- Ensure you are linked in to their retrospective outcomes. Every team should be creating action plans and will have things they need from leadership to succeed. Make sure you are solving these issues while you are visiting the global offices.

- Build working agreements that support core hours for availability, or alternative solutions for quick turnaround of feedback. Working agreements are mandatory among team members, especially when teams are split across geographies. Make sure your teams have them and adhere to them.

- Trade or share the burden of dealing with broad time-zone differences. We have used many different techniques to ensure the time-zone burdens are shared. Have meeting times change to be convenient for one team one week and the other team the next week. Pick a time that affects each team just a little (early morning for one and late evening for another). Share this burden to develop a real team mentality.

Better Yet, Eliminate Distributed Teams

Nearly everyone we talk to says this isn't a choice for them, yet if they knew the amount of waste built into the distributed delivery model, they'd realize the irony of thinking it's saving them cost and providing a value. The realization of the full cost is one of the main reasons we see for the pendulum swinging back to where teams are colocated.

Mitigate distributed teams as much as possible by having full execution teams at each location. We constantly see companies sending a portion of their execution teams offshore. This seems very popular with the QA portion of teams. Using this model sets up your organization for finger pointing and inefficiencies. It allows your engineers to disown the quality of their work. It puts the quality of your products in the hands of one team. Agile is all about the entire team owning the work, including the quality of that work. Allowing a part of the team to be in a different location undermines this principle. The most effective and efficient companies end up having as many full teams as possible in each location. It can take more than a year to get the right people on board at each location and to get some retraining completed, but it is well worth the effort.

When you do have to have a significant portion of the teams in a different location, send team members to the other location for extended periods of time. We sent engineers to the QA location for three to four months so they could integrate better with the quality team members. We sent quality team members to sit with the engineering teams for five to six months so we could advance automation and align the teams. It's harder for teams to finger point and blame other team members when they have met them and know them well.

There are quite a few studies you can find online that will help you justify the investment in a nondistributed delivery model. Either put the whole team in one location and solve the feedback loop problem or put them all in the same time zone. Direct cost might increase, but so will quality, productivity, and predictability; in addition, time to market, waste, and indirect costs will decrease.

Lack of a Transformation Product Manager

In many organizations, we find that there is a real understanding of the need for a product manager role. As we develop products, we know we need someone to oversee the entire profit and loss of the product line. We understand their role and that they have a deep knowledge about their markets, customer needs, and how to gain the most value for the company.

When we go about transforming the entire company, however, we expect this to just happen on its own. Some companies leave it up to a grassroots effort, and still others exclaim that they will "become Agile" and expect it to happen on its own.

Do you see the problem? It really makes no sense to believe that transforming your entire corporation can be done haphazardly, in people's spare time, as their interest dictates, and yet expect to have real outcomes that affect your organization.

- Is there consistency across your organization in practice and principle?
- Do people take ownership?
- Do you have fundamental corporate-culture issues?
- Who owns the transformation?

Does your organization look the same no matter where we drop in and look, or are there different practices and philosophies? In many organizations, the leadership believes they have to let the developers choose how they want to work, what tools to use, and what best practices to adopt. For an organization to be successful today, though, you need detailed data to run your business.

Having consistent portfolio, project, initiative, feature, story, defect, test case, and test run result data across all teams means that you need some consistent practices to which all teams adhere and you need them to track data in a consistent format so you can roll up the results.

Having a common definition of done for stories, iterations, features, and releases is important. It doesn't need to be exhaustive, but instead serves a baseline to which all teams are held accountable. Just like you have always had release criteria, you now have story, iteration, and feature criteria.

Best practices are important to define across all teams. Just like the definitions of done, these practices should not be heavy but should provide guidelines for how products are created and completed at your company.

What are the most important things that you do as a company? Create products for sale, reduce costs, and keep the business running. You need a consistent understanding and definition for the processes and practices you use to do these things, and consistent data must be part of the outcome.

Drop in on different areas of your organization and see if you see similarities in how they work.

- Congruency evidences itself through changes in behaviors across the team.

- Congruent team members move away from a yes–no, black–white, or us–them mentality.

- Congruent teams abide by norms in which pathological (yes, we said pathological) behaviors are not acceptable, because relationships matter.

The pathologies of blaming or placating are replaced with an emphasis on equal stature and equal voice. In environments of congruency, each member is heard, understood, and valued. Imagine your transformation as a product, but not software or a service you would sell. Rather, this product is one that works "on" your business. Your transformation product manager is the scout leader delivering a high-quality transformation.

This role works in a tight relationship with the executive owner of the transformation. Together, they define the disciplined exploration and execution to deliver a world-class transformation. They must be the models of congruence among all players in the transformation. They help the teams be attentive to the incongruent behaviors that can eat away at the sense of "us" and "we."

If you walk around your teams and notice tendencies toward pathological behaviors like blaming, placating, distracting, or being overly focused on process and structure, you are smack in the middle of incongruence. Ignore these harmful behaviors at your own risk. How can we better behave as a whole system to bring about the best results? Ensure your transformation product manager has the vision and empathy to recognize the destructive, incongruent behaviors and the skills and knowledge to fix them.

There must be a nonnegotiable value of trust, not just within a team, but across teams. Incongruent product owners focus on "what's in it for me." There is a protectionist attitude about their particular backlog and the teams that work on them. Blaming others becomes their primary communication mode.

Instead, you should expect your product owners to value what this product brings and its projected cost and value, and make decisions based on what's best for the overall portfolio. Remember, Drucker said culture eats strategy for breakfast.

Failure to Create Fast Feedback

For every action, there is an equal and opposite reaction.

—Newton

The best-laid schemes of mice and men / go often askew.

—Robert Burns, from "To a Mouse, on Turning Her Up in Her Nest with the Plough" (1785)

We've been part of product development companies for decades. In all those years, we have found a few principles with which everyone seems to agree: Plans change, and everything we do causes something else to happen, whether intentional or unintentional.

The law of cause and effect fostered the idea of assembly lines, waterfall processes, and postmortems. All of these are sequential, predictable, repeatable processes. Software development is anything but sequential, predictable, or repeatable, so we need to have frequent feedback loops.

In manufacturing, feedback loops on quality were less important or nonexistent compared to how many items came off the line at any given point. The nature of knowledge work is inconsistent with the predictable, sequential work Newton helped foster. We have to inspect to get feedback on bad behaviors or missed designs quickly and adapt.

Here are some examples:

- Clinging to a strict sense of predictability for when feature work will be completed.
- One centralized organization deciding all standards and rules for every team at the start of the transformation.

- Large-batch delivery of feature sets.

- Holding onto the belief that precision in analysis can resolve all risks in product delivery. We find that it is better to be roughly right than precisely wrong.

- Lack of experiments to test cause-and-effect assumptions about time, effort, and value.

- Blaming between business and development about delivery predictions and actual dates to support projected value.

- Blaming between development and testing about defects long after the features have been built.

- Failure to get feedback through retrospectives, or the retrospectives produce those pathological behaviors.

Fast feedback is the unspoken hero of congruency. We seek feedback on guesses (estimates), value, behavior, risk, culture, and Agile practices.

We look for feedback not only from our external customers, but from all of those involved in the transformation of your organization to a more modern way of working. We want feedback from team members, managers, directors, and all other levels of management. We want feedback from your natural leaders, whether they are management or not. All departments and all business units should be giving feedback.

Healthy Agile transformations crave fast feedback on every aspect of how the transformation is progressing. For this to occur, ensure you deliver feedback both ad-hoc and on a cadence, the latter being more formal and facilitated. Trust must be a fundamental part of your organization for you to get real feedback. Be sure to not give negative feedback to those making suggestions or those who mention things that are not working.

Ad-hoc feedback reduces the waste of waiting for direction on very transactional decisions; cadenced retrospectives ensure regular inspect-and-adapt sessions across the organization.

Shortchanging Collaboration and Facilitation

We are constantly playing with the balance of how to be a team member and how to remain an individual. This happens in all areas of an organization, from frontline engineers to C-level executives. Collaboration and teamwork is discussed as preferred, but we still need to stand out to get ahead.

Every day we struggle with balancing how to speak up, be valued, and not be afraid of recrimination while working toward the good of everyone. This is where a sense of congruency can help.

We are similar but all different and we need to facilitate our meetings in a way that lets everyone's voices be heard, regardless of the type of meeting or the level of people involved. The success of each meeting can hinge on how well each person was heard and how much their ideas were acknowledged.

When we don't facilitate well we create distrust in the team. People feel left out or that they aren't being heard. Facilitation is a skill that good Scrum masters should have. Being a good Scrum master requires more than just taking a two-day class. They also need to be great facilitators so they can integrate diverse perspectives to converge on actionable decisions. *The Five Dysfunctions of a Team* by Patrick Lencioni is a great read on this subject.[2]

To be clear, collaboration does not mean groupthink. Let team members disagree. We need to hear every perspective, and at times argue our points, so that we uncover risks, opportunities, puzzles, and surprises. Some of the best collaborative efforts we have participated in included quite a few arguments. From our perspective, people argue about something they are passionate about. If they don't care, they let someone else's opinion win. You want your teams to have passion about what they are doing. This leads to better products and outcomes, and usually to stronger teams.

We've all heard the statement that we are only as strong as our weakest link. The same holds true for voicing opinions: We are only as smart as the least vocal person on the team.

Failure to Transform Beyond IT

We hear many people talk about the reasons they want to take their company through an Agile transformation. These often include faster time to market, building things faster, improving quality, and meeting the demands of a fast-paced market. They expect their IT or products organization to carry the burden of making this happen.

We were working with one company who had brilliantly transformed their development teams. The teams focused on value, and delivered things more quickly and with higher quality. They actually completed a product that could completely disrupt their market before any of their competition. They couldn't get it into the market, though. The marketing department didn't know how to market it. The sales department didn't know how to sell it. The product sat on the shelf for four or five months so the rest of the company could catch up. During that time, a startup released a very similar product and beat them to market. They lost their disruption advantage. They lost a lot of revenue. They lost.

---

[2]Patrick Lencioni, *The Five Dysfunctions of a Team* (San Francisco: Jossey-Bass, 2002).

Transformation is about organizational change management. Change involves humans and sometimes humans are complicated. You need to address time, safety, and direct experience required to guide us through change or fail. You need to expand the transformation beyond your development teams or else it really doesn't matter how fast they move.

How are you tending to your sense of change—not just as steps in a process, but as humans and teams in transition?

When we leave the human context behind—when we ignore the time, safety, and direct experience required to guide us through change—we have failures in transition.

The perspective of many executives is to build it faster and get it to market faster, but we can't be successful simply by having a product ready. It's a whole system problem, not an IT problem. You cannot take the mandate approach we discussed earlier, nor can you simply throw more people at the problem.

You must address the root problems your company is having to succeed. Many executives come from the perspective of looking at how to build products faster and get to market faster, with more innovation, by making their engineering teams more efficient.

Speeding up value delivery by concentrating your transformation on product development is suboptimal. Concentrating Agile transformation in the development organization looks slick. They get a sense of speedy efficiency around them, and that's enticing. It can grab the hearts of people who thrive on heroics. Testers, developers, and UX are "transformed" into a new way of working across the product teams.

Through their work, the product engine begins to attain the purr of feature delivery. Is this truly transformative, though? No. Instead, look at the system as a whole to solve the real problems.

- Declaring the transformation from the executive level is insufficient.

- Rolling out all teams at once is insufficient.

- Starting up teams randomly is insufficient.

- Training everyone at once is insufficient.

Each of these is a useful but ultimately ineffective action, leaving the transformation sputtering toward a "good enough for now" end state. An Agile transformation is far bigger than the efficiency of delivery teams; it needs to encompass your entire organization and go well beyond IT.

Failure to Focus on People

We all have been part of companies that had us follow a process that had no benefit. We had to fill out templates or create metrics that either had no value to the business or that people used to make poor decisions.

In many organizations, we see people who view Agile practices as simply a replacement for the waterfall processes. Nothing could be further from the truth. Agile is not just about checking boxes and filling in templates. It involves teams, people, and their feedback in your transformation and how they work with each other and with you.

We cannot simply apply practices and measures and think we are Agile, and if that doesn't work apply more practices and measures. No amount of process will stop bad behaviors. The bottom line, though, is that Agile is not just about process and structure.

In many waterfall processes that we used we could check off all the boxes but not check in with the people. We threw documents over the silo walls to other groups and expected them to get everything they needed from those often hundred-page documents. Now we know that communication is key—that anything written down is a placeholder for a conversation.

We need to fundamentally change the way we do business with each other. How does the transformation lead teams to engage with their colleagues in defining success beyond practices and metrics? If we simply apply these practices and measure these things, surely success will come, but it never does. Then when success doesn't occur, we apply more process, right?

Ignoring the Path of the Individual

Every transformation requires that an organization move through a journey that is well described in the Kubler-Ross change curve. Figure 2-1 is a simulation of the phases Kubler-Ross described for grief, but they have been aligned to the phases people go through for change as well.

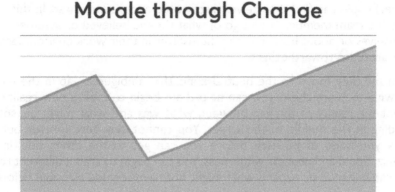

Figure 2-1. Phases of morale during change

We have seen executives who don't understand that change curve and allow teams to abandon the change before they reach the other side of the curve. They then deem Agile to be a failure and determine that it makes teams miserable. Nothing could be further from the truth. Teams are simply going through the standard change curve. Any change to the way they work will cause this. Any major change to your organization will cause it. Push through to the other side of the curve before you determine the validity of any change.

While teams are moving through this change, we cannot ignore the path of the individual. Change can create fear, uncertainty, and doubt whether you are changing processes, team members, or leadership. We tend to ignore the work of transition for each individual affected by the transformation.

There's always someone who has something to lose, whether true or imagined. For example, many midlevel managers fear they will be out of a job if agility takes hold. They put up roadblocks to adoption of Agile practices and tend to continuously point out how the new way of working is not valuable in the organization.

Directors who've attained their stature through their ability to push through adversity are now being asked to find their significance in how they guide and serve, not push. Heroes who save the day at the end of every project or release are losing their motivation as they're incentivized to work collaboratively in support of the team and at a sustainable pace. Teams are asked to alter their composition and perhaps their highly guarded bond. The well-meaning goal of creating a better way of working generates the unintended consequence of a big pile of fear, uncertainty, and doubt.

Human psychology is an interesting thing. People in transition shift from we to me. People can find themselves disoriented and disenchanted. In this stage, we guide team members to let go of what they've believed or assumed about themselves or about how they see themselves in their work environment and their attitudes toward others.

From me they move to the neutral zone, that ambiguous gap in the middle. Knowing they are there, you can help them begin to craft a new reality. We accept the reality of the gap between what was and what might be, sort of standing in the middle of the street. You cannot stay here forever, but you know you need to be here before you can get to the other side. In this organizational and process wilderness, you can begin to craft a different reality that can enhance or expand what might not have seemed plausible before.

Failure to Work from Backlogs

Backlogs are simply lists of work that has to be done. They are special lists because they are prioritized—not just high, medium, and low, but ordinally prioritized (1, 2, 3, 4)—so that when something is reprioritized, it affects the items that came before and after it.

Organizations that don't work from backlogs often find that they prove out the Standish Group study that says 60% to 80% of all features implemented are rarely or never used.[3] Think about that for a moment: 60% to 80% of the work that teams developing software do is simply waste.

Although the study was for four software products at four different companies, when I used to run QA departments I would determine which areas of our systems were used most frequently so I could do risk-based testing. I found these statistics to be pretty on point. The majority of users used about 20% to 30% of any product I tested, and some portions of the product (generally about 30% to 40%) were literally used by no one. Why is that? Because organizations don't organize work into backlogs. They use requirements documents. Requirements documents have been used since software was first created, so why are they a problem? Because they force the business to ask all at once for what they want. Because they aren't sure what they will actually need and they only get to ask once, they list everything they might need. Ability to print checks? Add it. Ability to send an e-mail to Mars (don't know if we will need it, but we might)? Add it, and so on.

---

[3]Jim Johnson, Chairman of the Standish Group, Keynote, "ROI: It's Your Job," Third International Conference on Extreme Programming, Alghero, Italy, May 26–29, 2002.

Basically, here's what happens. The business prints out a huge document that no one has read and certainly no one understands and gives it to the development teams. "Here's what we want you to build," they say. The programmers lug the huge document into their programmer cave and begin to do programmer things. Because requirements documents are part of predictive models (waterfall), the programmers might not actually speak to the business for six months, one year, or more. They are just busy programming and checking off items from the requirements document. Finally, late and over budget, they come out of the programmer cave and say, "Behold, the greatest piece of software ever written! It's bug free, it's highly optimized, and we wrote it in *Turbo Coffee COBOL Sharp+* because we thought you'd think that was cool. Here's your application."

The business takes one look at what's been written and says "Um, what is this?"

To which the offended programmers reply, "It's what you wanted, it's written right here in the requirements document."

Then the business utters the words that all programmers dread: "Well, that's not what we meant. We cannot use this."

Then the magical process known as change control begins.

Acknowledgment of Jean Tabaka's Influence   Much of this section was learned from and inspired by the late Jean Tabaka and her blog series. Jean was the author of *Collaboration Explained*[4] and an Agile Fellow at CA Technologies. Jean inspired untold numbers of people that she touched with her many gifts.

Jean taught me about Agile way back in 2003. We embarked on a never-ending journey to discover what these principles meant to a company and how we could change how we do business simply by applying these principles to all we do. Jean was a remarkable teacher, mentor, and human being, and she is greatly missed. —Laureen Knudsen

---

[4]Jean Tabaka, *Collaboration Explained* (Upper Saddle River, NJ: Addison-Wesley Professional, 2006).

Where's My Flying Car?

When we were young, we were promised a flying car. If all of this Agile stuff is true, why aren't all companies great by now and why is Doug still stuck driving in Dallas traffic instead of buzzing around in his flying car?

There are times when it seems like consultants and experts tell executives that to succeed today you have to become Agile. Be more nimble. Respond to the market and the changes therein. Then they walk away. It's like saying, "Flying cars are the way of the future, so you should really make your current car fly," and then walking away. No instructions are given, and the consultants don't have experience for how to get to the goal state.

However, there are proven ways to bring a traditional company through transformation to full agility. Let's look at some of the things we need to think about along the way.

Globalization vs. Innovation

- Globalization is simply copying what works elsewhere, aping a process in hopes it will work for you, without truly adopting or understanding it (e.g., "doing Agile").

- Innovation is creating something new that creates value. Creating value is not enough, though. You must also capture some of the value you create (e.g., "being Agile").

© CA 2018
D. Dockery and L. Knudsen, *Modern Business Management*,
https://doi.org/10.1007/978-1-4842-3261-3_3

Many times, in companies that are not realizing the benefits of more efficient and effective ways of working, we see a false adoption of Agile: teams defining Agile as a way to not have to plan, or teams insisting that agility means there cannot be a release date defined in advance. This is not, nor has it ever been, what Agile practices teach. Allowing teams to do whatever they want with no guidelines or standards is not Agile, nor is it any other methodology. Being Agile means as an executive, you have the information about the work being done that you need to understand what is really going on in your company, so you can respond to external forces. Good solid practices and data are naturally part of agility.

How Outlook Affects Adoption

In the most dysfunctional organizations, signaling that work is being done becomes a better strategy for career advancement than actually doing work.

As you will see in a later chapter, we worked with an organization where prioritization was a dirty word. Doing little bits of work on all projects kept teams from getting yelled at and allowed them the defense of "we're working on it" when asked for status.

We see, especially in really large companies, IT departments that are given huge budgets and told to do all the work at once. This makes no sense. We know that limiting work in progress allows teams to be more productive and that context switching wastes time. Yet we constantly see companies planning for wasted efforts and lack of progress against key projects. This is another way many executives are fooling themselves into thinking things are getting done when they are not. What are "process only" organizations really saying about themselves?

Minimum Viable Product and Iteration

Minimum viable product (MVP) and iteration are great concepts for improving a product, but most firms don't use them that way. They try to iteratively grow and use "Agile" as something to hide behind.

We have seen and been part of organizations that use MS Project templates as checklists to make sure everything is done in a release. They add in the specific tasks for the current features. These project plans can be hundreds, if not thousands, of lines long. We have seen them printed out and lining meeting room or hallway walls, often stretching on for years.

We walked into one company and they were so proud of their plans. They had planned out, in detail, how they were going to innovate over the next five years. They had their one-year, three-year, and five-year plans mapped out in Gantt charts and taped to the walls. There was even an architectural diagram that went along with it to show the tech stack they would use.

Anything that varied from the plan had to go through a tedious change control process. We gently asked if they planned to take advantage of, or incorporate into their products, technology that would be created in 18 months, two years, or 36 months, and how that was accounted for in their plans. In other words, did they plan for any change to happen at all?

In today's fast-changing markets, where disruption can happen at any time, how successful do you think this company will be? We doubt they would survive to see the five-year plan play out. Not only were they making unreal plans; they were spending time and money creating plans that could not possibly be real and would never come to fruition. This effort is primarily wasted time, money, and effort that could be applied to creating something that your customers would find valuable today.

Any company that tells you they know what their industry will be like in five years is kidding themselves and wasting precious resources on things that will be thrown out.

How many plans have you thrown out during the past year or two? How many hours were spent by your architects, principal developers, and top product managers on plans for features that would never be done? How many executives sat in meetings to review these plans and approve them? How much did those meetings cost? Add up the price for the plans and the meetings and be realistic with yourself. It's time to stop pretending that these things have any value to your organization. Following these types of processes is killing your business and allowing your competition to beat you to market with the things your customers really want today.

Greatness Is Not Incremental

Achieving greatness isn't incremental, nor is it for the faint of heart.

—Angela Tucci, CEO, Apto

We often hear that something that is easy is said to not be rocket science or brain surgery (or rocket surgery?). One of the stories we would like to share with you is about a company that quite literally does rocket science.

When you think of an organization changing to become more Lean or more Agile, what is the vision you have in your head? Teams of amazing coaches encouraging people to think differently about how work is done in their organizations? Well-thought-out presentations about the three-year plan to change an organization's culture? White papers written by the Agile world's best and brightest? Tearing down cubicles and replacing coffee with morning yoga? How about knowing that your current approach isn't working and being in month nine of an 18-month project where the future of your entire company is on the line?

That's the story of our rocket scientists. They were in the middle of a traditional project when they realized they were not going to meet their goals. They needed to do something drastic so they jumped right into replanning the project using Agile methods and bringing everyone together who was responsible for working on the project. They didn't incrementally begin doing certified Scrum master classes for each team. They didn't decide to only work with their mobile development team (or web or the other culprits that many organizations start and end with). They brought us in and literally jumped into being a fully Agile organization—even before they were 100% sure what that meant—and used the benefits that true transformation brings to organizations to reclaim the leadership position in their industry. The result? They finished their project on time, launched their rockets on time, and ended up winning their market.

That's great. Rocket surgery! But I don't do rocket surgery, I work in an insurance company or a health care company or a bank, so stories about rockets just don't describe what I do. So how about a very traditional bank that did the same thing?

A big-three auto manufacturer made an offer to a small, unknown bank: Scale to support us in three months and we will allow you to service our car leases. Imagine having to create a new product and services in three months. If you were successful, imagine that new product providing $60 million to your organization. Would that be worth trying something different? Now imagine that new product would provide $60 million per month. Would you be willing to try different things in a quest to be successful?

If both high-tech companies that work with rockets and very traditional banks can both take advantage of Lean or Agile transformations to change the way they work and affect the value that they create, what's the common denominator? The commonality is organizations that have innovative spirits, not just for incremental improvements that are delivered because of specific innovation, but exponential innovation that literally changes a market segment.

As a good rule of thumb, innovation must be ten times better than its closest substitute in some important dimension to lead to a real advance. Anything less than an order of magnitude will be perceived as an incremental, marginal improvement and will not move the needle. Organizations that truly adopt Lean or Agile transformational change see massive improvements and innovation. It's not uncommon for organizations to achieve 250% increases in productivity.

Let's look at how a study proves out the increases in quality, productivity, predictability, and responsiveness.

The Impact of Agile Quantified

There are some definitive findings that came out in a study of Agile projects done in 2014 by CA Technologies. They looked at nonattributable data from more than 160,000 projects, 50,000 Agile teams, and 13,000 active teams and found that you can make great gains just by having your teams stay stable (same people and focus). Stable teams are associated and correlate with:

- 60% better productivity
- 40% better predictability
- 60% better responsiveness

The study found that by simply dedicating people to one team, with one focus at a time, productivity was improved by 100%. In other words, people who were only dedicated 50% of the time were only half as productive as those who were dedicated 95% of the time or more. Studies show that people who work on more than five projects have very little actual productivity. Think back to the company we mentioned previously that was starting all IT projects at the start of each fiscal year. They had tens of projects going on concurrently, many using the same people. How much less productive were those teams than the ones who can focus and actually get work done?

Can you imagine doubling, tripling, or quadrupling your productivity simply by creating stable teams in your organization and flowing work to those teams? Making these types of changes can be the difference between you winning or losing the market.

Quality, predictability, and responsiveness were also all greatly improved for dedicated teams (Figure 3-1).

Figure 3-1. Benefit of dedicated teams

To achieve the most gains, you need to set teams and keep them consistent, making changes as infrequently as possible. A trend we see is for companies to create teams, but to change the members of the teams, or pull people off of teams to create new teams every quarter. The statistics show that 25%, or one out of four people change teams each quarter. That creates a lot of churn and decreases productivity, quality, predictability, and responsiveness. Set your teams and keep them as consistent as possible for maximum gains.

This is why you see many consultants telling companies to flow work to the teams instead of forming teams around work. Most executives don't understand the real benefits of doing so or how to do this effectively, however.

How would you like the quality of your products improved by 250%? This same study showed that teams that follow full Scrum estimation processes (points on stories, and hours on tasks) had a 250% improvement in defect density than those that did no estimations, and a marked improvement over those that followed a Lightweight Scrum methodology (story point estimation only), or those that estimated only in hours on tasks (Figure 3-2).

Quality

Defects by Process Choice

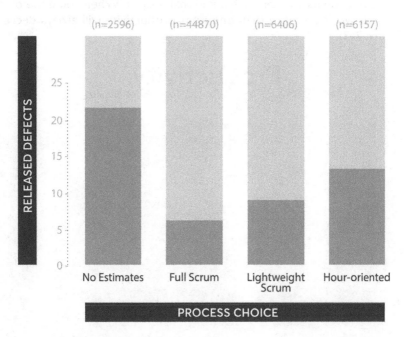

Figure 3-2. Defects by process choice

If your teams are relatively new to Agile, or you aren't seeing these types of benefits, make sure they are doing disciplined Agile practices. After a team has been together for a while, they can use a lighter-weight Scrum methodology and be even more successful. However, we believe the statistics that show improvement when using lightweight scrum are for advanced teams who have been working together in the same way for months.

- Experienced teams get best results from Lightweight Scrum.
- If new to Agile, are not seeing the benefits of agility, or are more strongly focused on quality, choose Full Scrum.

The study also focused on time to market. Almost every customer we talk to mentions that they need to get more done, faster, and get product into the market more quickly. Limiting the amount of work a team does at once can have a dramatic effect on how fast you get something to market.

If your company is one that rewards those that seem overly busy, now is the time to stop that practice. We can't tell you how many people we talk to in companies that pride themselves on having 11 projects going at any given time for the same team. What this immediately tells us is that nothing is getting done. Context switching wastes time and effort. Different studies show slightly different amounts of time and effort wasted but the average is ~20% loss of productivity for each additional project. When someone on the team has to work on more than one item, productivity will always decrease (see Figure 3-3).

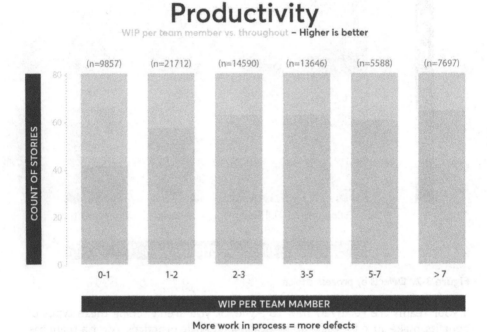

Figure 3-3. Less WIP equals faster time to market

As an added bonus, teams with the lowest work in progress (WIP) have four times better quality than teams with the highest WIP. WIP is the measure of the number of simultaneous work items that are in process at the same time.

It seems logical that the fewer things a team works on at a time the faster each item will be completed, but if there are too few items in the queue, productivity can decrease by up to 34%. There is a happy medium for each team on the best number of items that can be worked at any one time. Some believe the best place to start is 1 item per team member +1. So, the items in progress at any one time would never be more than 1 per person on the team +1. The +1 accounts for any wait time that might be needed and keeps team members working.

If your WIP is already high, then by all means drive it lower. However, if your WIP is already low, consider your economic model before you decide to drive it lower. If you're at risk for missing a market window, then drive your WIP as low as possible by focusing on just a few things. If productivity is the primary driver of your economic model, however, don't push your WIP to extremely low levels because if work gets blocked, your teams won't have anything to work on.

This is also why it's important to keep backlog items prioritized. If teams become blocked for current work, they can pick up something from the backlog to work on. There should always be the "next thing" that needs to be done. These top backlog items need to be fully fleshed out and ready to be worked on.

Controlling your WIP is also a way to speed time to market. We see a direct link between the number of items in progress and the time in process for each item. Queuing theory (Little's law in particular) predicts that there will be a linear relationship between the number of items in progress and time it will take to get them done. We can see this link in Figure 3-4.

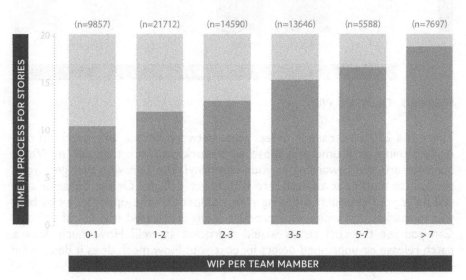

Figure 3-4. Responsiveness and WIP

The time in process for teams that poorly control their WIP is up to two times as long as it is for teams that control their WIP very well. This makes logical sense: The more focused you are on a few things, the quicker you'll get each one done.

Not surprisingly, there is also a relationship between the number of items in progress and the quality of our work (see Figure 3-5). The number of defects released with software is in direct correlation to the number of items in progress per person. The fewer items worked on at any given time, the fewer mistakes made.

Figure 3-5. Quality and WIP[1]

There is a 250% increase in defect rates between people who work on one or two things at a time and those who work on more than seven. Which behavior are you rewarding in your company? The behavior that gets your product to market at a faster rate with fewer defects? Or the behavior that will delay your products, allowing your competition the opportunity to beat you to market, and when your product finally is released, it is full of defects? Can you see the cost ratios would skyrocket as well? How much does a patch release or unplanned defect fix cost you? How much does it delay your current projects?

There are many other data points in the study "The Impact of Agile. Quantified," but the last one we talk about here is the retrospective and its impact on the work of the team.

---

[1]CA Technologies, "The Impact of Agile. Quantified," http://www.ca.com/content/dam/ca/us/files/white-paper/the-impact-of-agile-quantified.pdf, June 13, 2014.

Teams that do retrospectives and use them as a chance for continuous improvement have a higher performance rating than those that don't reflect on their work and on how they work. Teams that complete retrospectives have a 20% higher balanced performance than teams that don't conduct retrospectives (see Figure 3-6).

Sprint Retrospective Relationship to Performance

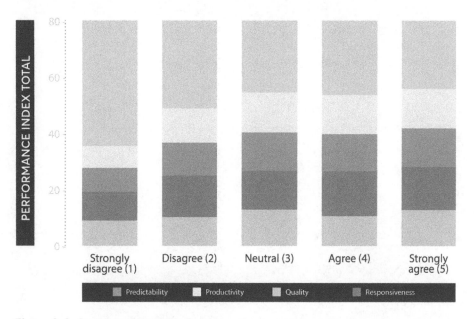

Figure 3-6. Retrospectives and performance

Consistent and effective retrospectives where learnings are applied for future improvement can significantly affect teams' performance in future sprints, yet we talk to so many people who don't see the need for them or don't want to complete them. It's not easy to review your own work with a critical eye, and retrospectives can often bring up topics that are uncomfortable to discuss. If your teams are not doing retrospectives this can indicate that they might also have a lack of communication and willingness to take on the hard issues affecting their performance. Make sure these teams are getting the coaching they need to overcome these issues.

Now let's examine how we understand where your company is on the spectrum and how you can meet your productivity, responsiveness, predictability, and quality goals.

Three Simple Questions

When we first meet with clients, we ask them three simple questions to frame our conversation. We would ask you to think about the answers to these questions for you, your teams, and your organization.

Tell Me About Your Teams

The first question we ask when meeting a new client or prospective client is "Tell me about your teams." We are hoping to learn is the following:

- How their teams are organized

- How large their teams are

- If their teams are working from a backlog or a requirements document

- How often they "deliver" value; for example, do they create value in two week cycles, once a month, or once a year?

- Where does the value they create go; for example, what are the environments that they have to navigate to get something from development to the customer (and how long does that usually take)?

© CA 2018
D. Dockery and L. Knudsen, *Modern Business Management*,
https://doi.org/10.1007/978-1-4842-3261-3_4

If they say that are Lean or Agile, then we'll ask these questions:

- How long their iterations or sprint is

- If they have people assigned to the product owner and Scrum master roles

- Who they invite to their sprint review (demo)

- How long their daily standup (morning meeting, daily Scrum, daily meeting, etc.) lasts and who attends

We always end by talking about how their teams continually get better. If they are working in a Lean or Agile way, we talk about their retrospectives; if not, we talk about lessons learned (or whatever they call it). If the client gets nothing else out of our conversation, we always hope they get this one item: Retrospect ruthlessly and retrospect often. It's the only way for a team to get better, and teams getting better is the only way an organization gets better. There are many different ways to do retrospection—the style is unimportant—the important thing is actually doing it. Even if it's as simple as "What is working," "What is not working," and "What are we going to do about it?," it's a critical part of the feedback loop that makes Lean or Agile work.

We use the questions to drive conversation, but also as a way of helping the organization discover (at least publicly) things about their teams. We focus on both potential positives and potential negatives during the conversation. Let's take a moment and run through the questions. Think about the answers for your organization, but also think about why knowing the answers is important if you're planning (or living!) your own Lean or Agile transformation.

How Are Your Teams Organized?

Do they work in silos or are they dependent on other teams to get things done? If they depend on other teams, are those teams working in the same way as your team? This means if your teams are Lean or Agile and they are working with teams that are using a predictive (waterfall) methodology, you will need to take into account the differences in how they are working when you plan. If your teams are Lean or Agile and work in a silo, we would suggest that you aren't getting very much value for the effort you put into transforming them. You've created an expensive hobby, but that really isn't what you set out to achieve, is it? The value and power of lean or Agile is in how the teams work with the larger organization. Silos are at odds with collaboration. We talk more in the next section, about how to fix this problem.

Are Your Teams Working From a Backlog or From a Requirements Document?

That seems like a really basic thing to want to know. Really, why does it matter? As long as they know the things that your customer or business partner wants, that's good enough, right?

Think for a moment about requirements documents. What are they really? Sure, they represent the work that someone (or a group of someones) wants your teams to create, but a requirements document is really a point-in-time list of everything anybody could think of that they might, maybe, possibly want someday. Why do we say it that way? Well, a requirements document is really an invitation to have one chance to ask for what you want a group of programmers to do. Because our business partners get one chance to ask for things, they ask for everything: They might need it and will not get to ask again, so they better include it, right? Major studies from Standish Group and IBM conclude that 60% to 80% of all requested features (things that end up in a requirements document) are rarely or never used. How does that manifest in real life?

The business puts everything they can think of in a requirements document. They think, "I only get to ask this one time, and I might need it, so I'm going to add it to the document. Do I really need to send SMS messages to Mars? Probably not, but let's ask for it."

The requirements document is then given to the programmers. The programmers take it and go into their programming cave and six months, one year, or maybe longer, later they emerge. Programmers coming out of the programming cave is generally accompanied by great fanfare: "Ta-da! Look at what we've built! This is the greatest work of programming in human history. The application we've crafted is highly efficient, optimized, and truly a wonder to behold." The programmers then deliver their opus to the business and stand there, with smug, expectant looks on their faces.

What do you think the business says when they receive the fruits of the programmers' labors? Usually something along the lines of "What the hell is this?" To which the programmers respond, "It's what you asked for. See? It's written right here." The business then responds with something truly astounding, like, "Well, that's not what we meant."

Working from a backlog is different. It allows the business partners to prioritize the work so that there is a rank-order list of things they want. The items with the most value to the customers are at the top. The business partners are given opportunity, every two weeks or so, to reprioritize this list. We don't recommend they do it every two weeks, as that would create a lot of churn, and outcomes with little value, but it can be done. Using a backlog removes the need to ask for everything you could ever want because you won't be able to ask again for a year. It also removes the impetus to make everything a "must have" like we see so frequently in requirements documents.

Let's think of the products your company creates. What if you could have your business people create a list of things they want the product to do (whether those things come from current customers, prospects, market analysis, or internal suggestions)? They prioritize that list based on how much the customers will value the item on the list. They can add to the list and rework the priority at regular cadences. Would that reduce the amount of your products that are rarely or never used? Would your customers value more fully a product that is filled with features they would actually use?

These are the benefits of working from a backlog rather than a requirements document that includes a wish list of items that customers might or might not want, but that the development team is expected to create.

How Often Do You Deliver Value?

You've heard, we're sure, of continuous delivery, where organizations release to the customer frequently. Unfortunately, many Lean or Agile organizations don't practice continuous delivery, they practice occasional delivery, delivering to the customer one or two times per year. Their teams create incremental value, but it just piles up until the pile gets big enough that something has to be done with it, and it gets shoved through the final phases and into the customers' hands.

If using SaaS or Cloud environments, the process of moving code from a development environment into a production environment is complicated by the lack of discipline in development teams and by the number of environments needed between development and production.

In nonregulated environments, you might need to move the code from development to a QA environment, then on to usability testing, then to some sort of performance testing and finally to production. If your teams aren't disciplined, the number of times code is moved through these environments can be huge. We worked with a company that was moving from on-premises delivery to Software-as-a-Service (SaaS). Customers found a high-severity defect in one of the products in production. The team created a bug fix and had it moved to production that night (unfortunately, this product had a design flaw that required a service to be stopped and started each time an update was made to the product—which brought the entire environment down for all users). The fix didn't work. They redid it the following day to be uploaded that night. Again, there was an issue with the code. This went on for four or five days, and each time the entire system had to stop for all users so the service could be restarted.

Ninety percent of the customers affected by that bug fix were not even on the product that had the bug. The product they were using happened to sit on the same servers, so they were affected when the service was stopped and restarted every night. They received no benefit from the bug fix, because the bug hadn't affected them. They number of service calls received by that company increased each time they had to restart the service, and there was no good explanation to give to the customers who were affected.

Had the team doing the bug fix fully tested the fix in an environment that matched production, this could have eliminated the impact to the customers. Create the right processes and procedures and require that they be followed to ensure this doesn't happen to you.

We ended up reviewing the processes for the team causing the problem and got them the training, coaching, and knowledge they needed to eliminate the problem in the future. We also moved the story that eliminated the need to stop and restart the service each time the software was updated to the top of their backlog.

This is another reason that teams, especially Lean or Agile teams, need a professional, repeatable way to move code, test cases, test data, virtualized services, and so on, from environment to environment.

How Long Is Your Iteration or Sprint?

A sprint is a standard unit of time within which teams focus on creating value. The more uninterrupted time the team can have, the more productive they become. However, life also happens. Companies need to interrupt one or more members of the team. Other work needs to happen. All of these things need to be used to determine the length of a sprint or iteration.

The sprint time frame is not just used by the team to get a unit of value completed, but it's also a time during which the company agrees to leave the team alone. Can you not interrupt the team for more than two weeks? This means no demo setup, no estimations for unplanned work, and no management tasks. The rest of the company agrees to let the team focus on their planned work without interruption.

How far out can your employees know what will happen in their lives? Unexpected things occur all the time, but we try to set the time boxes in small enough chunks that you can predict well enough what will happen. I can probably predict what will happen in the next two weeks, but things become fuzzier when I think out a month. Generally, vacation time and days off are planned more than two weeks in advance.

For most companies and teams, the correct answer is usually two weeks. We see teams setting sprints at three or four weeks when they don't want to spend the time breaking down their work into manageable chunks. This is an indication that an antipattern to good Agile practices is occurring and should be reviewed by coaches or management who understand the needs of the company, team, and best practices to help the team make the final determination.

Do You Have People Assigned to the Product Owner and Scrum Master Roles?

Are these people skilled in the work that needs to be done in these roles? We see companies put low-skilled people into these roles all the time and then not understand why the wrong things are being created or their customers aren't seeing the value in the products. These roles take skills. The most successful product owners we have seen were formerly product managers. In some companies, they call them technical product managers, as they can take the information from the market analysis and determine the enhancements needed to give the customer a product they want to use, and more importantly, buy.

Companies often try to take project managers or program managers and turn them into Scrum masters. Sometimes this works, but more frequently it does not. Program and project managers generally run their projects by command and control; they drive their teams to get projects done. Being a Scrum master is a completely different role. It's a coaching and mentoring role. The Scrum master should know more about Agile practices than the rest of the team and should be constantly striving for improvements to how the team is working. They also remove impediments to success for the team, whether that means working with the team on behavior modification, working with others in the organization to remove a blocking factor, or bringing the hard conversations up to leadership and management to help the teams be more productive.

We were working at a company where the teams in three different product lines were being affected by the slowness of their QA environment. No one alerted anyone in management to ask for capital so they could replace the machines. Instead, the project managers just pushed the teams to work more hours to get projects completed on time. The teams were burning out and a few team members found other roles and moved on.

It took five months for someone to mention to the vice president, who could sign for the capital expense, that new servers were needed. There was no issue with the money being spent—there was capital budget available. Because the project managers were not Scrum masters, though, and they were used to driving the teams to get work completed rather than removing impediments, three product lines suffered. It was not the low performers who left to find other roles, but rather the highly prized superstars who were able to quickly move out of a poorly functioning team.

Make sure you have the right people in the roles and that they understand their new roles and how to be successful. Simply moving a group of people into a new role and giving them a two-day Scrum master training class is not a recipe for success.

We also see where companies have a shortage of workers in these roles. Determine the value of the product owner and the Scrum master to your organization prior to moving people into these roles. Then determine who fits into it best. Some of the best Scrum masters we've seen have come from engineering or QA. Some of the best product owners have been former product managers or business analysts.

Who Do You Invite to Your Sprint Review (Demo)?

One of the key tenets of agility is openness and transparency. Organizations realize this tenet in different ways. Everybody who cares about the outcome of the sprint should attend the demo. It's imperative that this be the entire Scrum team, but should also include members of other teams who might have dependencies on what is created or who might be creating something similar. This can also be other product managers, product owners, or Scrum masters who want to see how other teams are operating. It can also be executives who have a vested interest in the value being created. It can also include customers—real customers—who can give input on whether the right thing is being created.

In other words, everyone who wants to attend should be invited to the sprint demos. Determine the best way for the attendees to give feedback and make sure the meetings are facilitated so the discussion stays relevant. Use the Parking Lot method or other ways to table conversations that everyone in the room doesn't need to be a part of.

Your sprint demos can be extremely valuable meetings within your organization and can be the bridge between Scrum teams, the business and the team, the customer and the team, and between executives or leadership and the teams.

How Long Do Your Teams' Daily Standups (Morning Meeting, Daily Scrum, Daily Meeting, etc.) Last and Who Attends?

Do you ever walk the halls of your engineering groups and see them having their standup meetings? You can tell a great deal about the health of a Lean or Agile transformation by attending the daily standup and seeing whether groups hold each other accountable.

The daily meeting is where each person on the team tells the rest of the team their plan for the day and whether they met the previous day's plan. These are not status meetings. They are planning meetings. The team should be talking about their work against their sprint plan, if they are on track to be successful with completing the work they committed to for the sprint. If someone is falling behind or needs help, they tell the rest of the team and it is the team's responsibility to meet the commitment.

We see issues where each team member believes he or she is responsible for his or her piece of the work only. A sprint plan commitment is made by the entire team and they all agree that the work can get done. The team members start policing themselves and making sure someone on the team isn't taking on more than he or she can complete. If one person on the team doesn't meet his or her commitment, the entire team fails. This is one way that teams start self-managing their work and themselves.

How Does Work Flow in Your Organization?

The second question we ask is "How does work flow in your organization?" More directly, this can be asked as "How does something go from an idea or something you must do, to approved, funded work in your organization?"

Many companies do their funding during an annual planning process. They determine their strategic goals and align funding to meet those goals. These can be called strategies, themes, initiatives, or epics; they have differing names in different companies but they mean the same thing: They're a big huge goal that needs to be met.

How do you decide what to fund? Is it based on value to the company? Value to your customers? Invest in those things that will make or save the company the most money or that will provide the most value. This seems logical, but we are surprised at how many companies don't prioritize based on outcomes.

So now you have these funded ideas, and they are given to teams to break down into two-week chunks of work so they can fit into a sprint or iteration. How does this happen in your organization? Do you give the work to product managers and hope for the best? Do you hire consultants to manage the strategies? How do your teams know what to work on first?

Generally, we are told that there are backlogs for the projects and the teams pull from the top of those backlogs for each sprint.

How Are the Backlogs Ordered?

Are they ordinally ordered, where there is one #1, one #2, one #3, and so on? Are teams told that everything is most important? The most successful teams have backlogs that are well groomed (an Agile term meaning each story is well written, with acceptance criteria, and prioritized in order of value). If your backlogs are not in this shape, if the stories are poorly written and don't include acceptance criteria, your teams are left to figure out what they are supposed to do to create some value. Teams will "fill in the blanks" to the best of their abilities, often getting you far from the place you want to be to optimize the value to those using the product.

Are Your Backlog Items Estimated?

How do you estimate the effort it will take to do the work? If you are still creating full specifications and design documents for every enhancement you are wasting precious resources: time, money, and people.

How Do You Plan?

The third question we ask is "How do you plan?" What we are really hoping to discuss is:

- Who is involved?
- How far out do you plan?
- What happens if the world you planned for changes?

Why does it matter who is involved in planning? Shouldn't it be obvious who should be involved? You just need the developers, maybe a project manager or two, and the QA folks, right?

Here's a story about planning that will illustrate the point. One of us used to be an enterprise architect in a previous life (we'll never tell which one, but it's not Laureen). Our architect worked on an initiative at a large financial institution to implement a remote deposit capture feature. Remote deposit capture is the idea of taking a photo of a check on your smartphone and being able to deposit it directly into your banking account. At the time this work took place, things like remote deposit capture were truly cutting-edge technology.

In any event, we worked on the initiative to deliver remote deposit capture, and delivered it on time and on budget. It was a really well written (and fantastically architected!) mobile application. It went into production and the app store flawlessly. It worked beautifully—for about two hours. You see, it does matter who is involved in planning, and we didn't invite the infrastructure team to our planning efforts. The new virtual servers that we had "planned" on were not installed because the infrastructure team didn't know they were needed. To make a long story somewhat shorter, the new back-end processing of images to turn pictures into checks ended up locking up some processors and eventually required a reboot of a transactional system that caused the ATM network to drop into "store and forward" mode for a short period of time. If you've ever worked in a financial institution, you know that doing anything to the ATM networks is not a very positive thing.

Now let's imagine a more positive alternative. What if we had brought all the teams that were affected by the implementation of this new functionality together to plan, work out dependencies (outside of production), and derisk the initiative. The outcome from that kind of inclusive planning seems like it would have been better, doesn't it?

We'll talk about inclusive planning in greater detail later, but it's one of the items we try to leave with teams. Planning in silos or in a vacuum is a recipe to "take down the ATM network" and that's something we want our clients to avoid.

Feral Teams, or Optimized to Execute

By now we're sure you've heard a great deal about Agile. You might even have some Lean or Agile teams in your company. Your firm probably started down the Lean or Agile path because someone went to a seminar and heard that Lean or Agile teams would:

- Be more efficient

- Create higher quality products

- Boost morale with their highly collaborative nature

Unfortunately, most of our customers find that they aren't getting what they expected from their investment into Lean or Agile. We see companies spending millions and millions of dollars on an Agile transformation and seeing little to no benefit from any of that spending. One of the biggest reasons for this is that there is no coordination to how teams are adopting Agile practices. Because management isn't being trained, they can't say how they want teams to work in this new methodology. The teams turn into what we call feral Agile teams. Each team of seven to nine people does whatever it wants in its pursuit of agility. The teams actually don't have to follow any Agile practices or standardized ways of working because they are "doing Agile." We are hearing that the Agile teams are a "black hole" and they aren't even required to attend biweekly status meetings that waterfall teams have to attend.

Needless to say, this is not Agile. This type of working environment is far removed from the goals of agility and from the benefits you should be getting.

It's not the teams' fault: People are going to take advantage of something if you let them. Make sure you are implementing solid, disciplined Agile practices, and collecting the rich data that comes from these practices, so your teams are optimized to execute (see Figure 4-1).

Team Execution

(Build it Right)

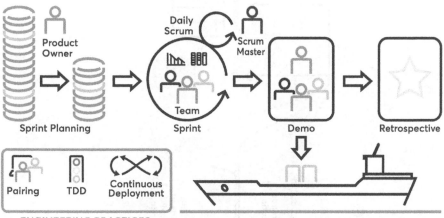

Figure 4-1. Team-level execution

Another issue we see is that teams are often building the wrong things because the company doesn't have a way to link strategy and execution. They've got a big hole—a chasm actually—in the middle of their organization. They try lots of ways to fill in the chasm but there is really only one way that works.

We've helped companies of all sizes, including *Fortune* 100 financial institutions, auto manufacturers, petroleum and chemical corporations, and retail organizations, as well as startups, to fill in their chasm and connect their strategic initiatives to the awesome Lean or Agile execution their teams represent. They've learned to invest in the right things, build them the right way, and most important, to build the right things at the right time to generate the most value from their development effort. That's the promise of Lean or Agile at scale, of truly becoming a Lean or Agile organization. We'll show you how to do it in the remaining chapters.

That Didn't Work, Let's Try This

Once we've demonstrated that team-level execution and a focus on engineering is not the answer to the problem of how to achieve business agility, many customers want to talk about how work flows to their teams. Most start with that annual festival when everyone looks forward to receiving gifts. Everyone receives them, more if you were good in the prior year, fewer if you were bad. No, we're not talking about Christmas; we're talking about annual planning.

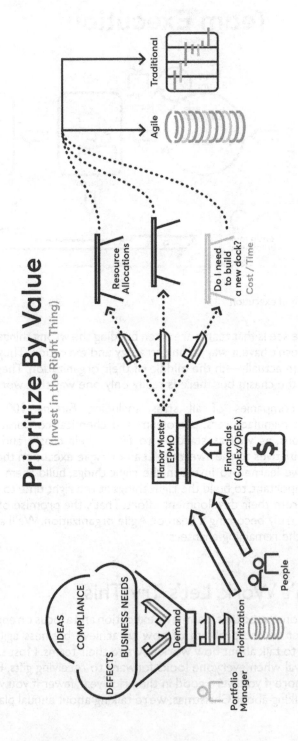

Figure 4-2. Invest in the right things

Prioritization by Value

Annual planning is making all the important decisions about what a company is going to build in the coming year, how much it's going to cost, and who is going to do the work at the very beginning of the planning cycle when you know the least about the work (see Figure 4-2). Further, it's a 12-month plan. The plans are made assuming that they will be valid three months, six months, and even nine months in the future. Our experience is that the world is constantly changing, so plans that extend that far into the future simply aren't that useful. Planning is critical. Long-term plans are at best educated guesses.

Annual plans also select, fund, and release all the projects for the coming year. Why is having all that work come out of the planning process and go into a backlog a good idea? Let's think for a moment about what happens if we do not use a backlog.

The best example we can give for this is a team from a *Fortune* 100 agricultural and construction equipment manufacturer that the first author led on an Agile transformation. He was asked to speak to a team that was having difficulty with Agile. He had not coached them and he didn't really know anything about the particular team, so he made an appointment to speak with them.

As he always does, he asked the three questions to find out about the team.

Question: Tell me about your teams.

Answer: We're using Scrum. We've been together for about two years. We're a business intelligence team. We feel like we do a great job of following the Scrum ceremonies and practice Agile well.

That sounded pretty good, so he wasn't sure what the problem was. He moved on to the next question.

Question: Tell me how work flows to your teams.

Answer: Well, you know how we plan here. Annual planning happened in January, and the projects that we were assigned were released to our team to work on. We were given 71 projects for this year.

Seventy-one? Because he didn't know about the specific work they had been asked to do, he wasn't sure if 71 was good or bad. He moved on to the third question.

Question: How do you plan?

Answer: We're really busy and our team's velocity is pretty standard from sprint to sprint. We estimate the work that is coming into the next sprint and then we commit to it during the sprint planning meeting.

He was really confused at this point. Everything he heard sounded pretty good, and he had run out of questions. However, as he continued to talk to them he eventually asked, "How many of the 71 projects that you were assigned have you finished this year?" As it was July, he thought this was sort of an important thing to know.

What do you think their answer was? Zero! Now we're getting somewhere.

Question: Zero? Why is it zero?

Answer: In our organization, it's more important to signal that work is being done than it is to actually finish anything. So, we work a little bit on each project each month.

Question: Why?

Answer: Because it's easier to work on all of them than to pick one and finish it. If we pick one, everyone else will yell at us for not working on their project. Nobody tells us what is most important.

Just for fun, he asked one more question.

Question: How many of the 71 projects that you got for this year are carry-overs from last year?

Answer: 68.

Let that sink in for a moment: 68 projects for an expensive business intelligence team were going on two years old. Just in case you were curious, they "planned" to actually finish none of the 71 projects they were working on.

None. Why is that? Because they failed to do two things. First, they didn't put work into a backlog and manage it. They simply released all the work and, essentially, drowned the team. Second, they didn't prioritize the work (whether in a backlog or not). They left it up to the team. We don't know about you, but we've worked in several places where priority was determined by such scientific methods as who the team likes best, who screams the loudest when their work doesn't get done, or what the team likes to do best. We're sure where you work wouldn't have that problem, right?

As with the team-level conversations, where we focused on building it right, there is a simple mantra for strategic planning: Invest in the right thing. Do not just invest in it, but make sure that what has been selected to be worked on is clear to everyone in your organization and that everyone understands the priority order in which they should be built. Collaboration about what to build, how to build it, dependencies, common risks, and timing is one of the most difficult things most organizations do. Only half of the companies we talk to address the need for real collaboration. Few do it well.

Even if you can successfully choose the right things to build and have a stellar team building them, you still have an additional problem to overcome. As we'll see in the next chapter, you have to deal with the chasm that exists in the middle of your organization.

Houston, We Have a Chasm

We recently met with a customer that had incredible strategies for where to take their company over the next five to ten years. They will be revolutionizing communications across the globe in ways we can't even imagine today. They felt their execution teams were building things well but they still struggled to determine how to complete their strategies. As with many other companies, they intended their strategy and execution plans to link, but there was a large disconnect. We call this the chasm, depicted in Figure 5-1.

© CA 2018
D. Dockery and L. Knudsen, *Modern Business Management*,
https://doi.org/10.1007/978-1-4842-3261-3_5

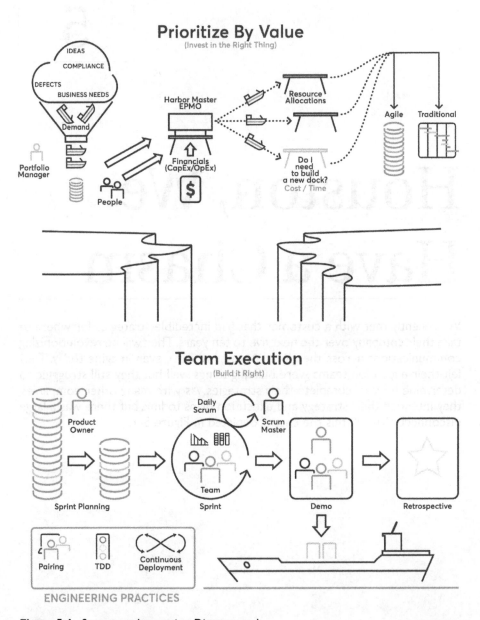

Figure 5-1. Strategy and execution: Disconnected

Many customers we talk to believe that if they can manage their investments and harness the awesome execution capabilities of Lean or Agile teams, then they have solved the problem and achieved the benefits of modern business management.

They are mostly right, except for the huge hole in the middle of their organization. They've got a chasm that separates their strategy from their execution. When we help them see the obvious disconnection, many immediately start to tell us "how" they are going to eliminate the disconnect or bridge the chasm and connect their organization's strategy and execution. There are three common answers to the disconnect and—spoiler alert—none of them will solve the problem.

The first answer we hear, usually from larger, more traditional organizations, is that they are going to use process to solve the problem. They say something like, "You're right. But we're going to become CMMI Level 4 compliant and standardize our processes and that will solve the problem." Unfortunately, process will not work. If it did, predictive models like waterfall would be fantastic and we all know that waterfall practices are leading to the issues we are trying to solve. The answer, therefore, isn't process.

The second answer we hear is tooling. Clients tell us that they are going to acquire or use a tool to solve the problem. Our response usually shocks them, and might surprise you as well. You see, we work for a company that makes and sells software products, and when we tell clients that purchasing a tool to try to bridge the chasm not only will not solve the problem, it will actually make it worse, they are generally rendered speechless. Injecting a new tool into an already bad process just gives the teams and their management something new to focus on, and to potentially blame when things go wrong.

"We would have delivered that project on time, but we were trying to learn how to use this new, complex tool, so unfortunately, we are later than we would have been otherwise. Don't blame us, Mr./Ms. Manager; you are the one that made us use this new tool." This is a pretty common outcome when organizations try to solve organizational and personnel problems with tools.

The third answer is near and dear to both our hearts. Clients tell us that they are going to hire consultants to solve the problem for them. Both of us have been consultants in past professional lives and when we see the chasm and hear that companies are going to try to solve it with consultants, it makes us think of movies we've all seen where a volcano is about to erupt and a person is thrown into the volcano to save everyone else. Clients are actually telling us that they are going to keep throwing consultants into the hole until it fills up and strategy and execution can be connected across the new pile of consultants. "Sacrificial" consultants not only sounds horrible, but using them will not work, either. Just as we read in the Agile Manifesto, we value certain things over other things. Neither are necessarily bad; we just believe one is more important. Consulting firms, in our experience, are no different. They value helping clients solve problems, but they value billable hours more. A strictly consulting solution will be a very expensive lesson in why organizational change is not something that a third party can, for an hourly rate, cause your organization to adopt.

As an aside, if you are going to hire consultants to help you transform, make sure they are actually using Agile practices. Many times companies have shown us the proposals the large consulting firms sent them: waterfall plans to roll out Agile! They literally show a waterfall of events through which they believe a company becomes Agile.

Instead, ask any company you plan to engage if they can let you see them practice what they preach. Can you swing by an office and see daily standup meetings happening? Can you see how they plan? Can you see the outcomes of the processes they are recommending? Can you see them in action? If you are going to give someone tens or hundreds of thousands of dollars to help you move toward agility, please make sure they use Agile practices themselves.

If none of those approaches works, what does? The next two sections describe a framework for success and an operational model that we have found works for organizations that have successfully made the leap to modern business management.

A Framework for Success

When adopting a framework, we need to take three things into consideration (Figure 5-2).

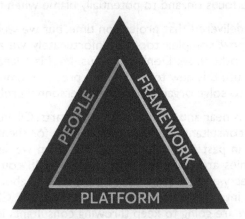

Figure 5-2. The transfomation triangle

- The people that we are attempting to transform

- The framework that will allow us to not constantly reinvent the wheel

- A platform to support the transformational efforts

People

When embarking on organizational change, the people that are to be transformed represent the most difficult and expensive portion of the transformation. People are complex and don't always react the way that we would like them to.

Transforming the people involves presenting them with a vision of a new way to do work. This vision values how work is done in a radically different way— it's no longer about "how we've always done things" but instead we prioritize doing work in the "right way" over just working. When we talk about the "right way" we mean:

- Working in small batch sizes.

- Getting completely done with things before you start something else.

- Proving that you are done and that you have created what your team committed to create.

- Working together and harnessing the power of your organization vs. that of a single team or individual.

- Constantly learning and continuously improving how we work by driving out inefficiencies.

You can see that there is nothing in this list that pertains to creating a product. These practices can be used throughout your entire organization to become more lean, effective, and efficient.

When you implement these types of practices at any level, the teams will go through the same phases of change that we referenced earlier. Also, issues will be highlighted and brought to the forefront so you can deal with them. Remember to push through these phases of change together and use the data that arise as an opportunity for learning rather than taking punitive measures.

When the practices become your new norm for working, the value each team provides will increase. Morale also increases, which is one of the things we never thought possible when we first started implementing Agile practices more than a decade ago.

One of the first companies where we implemented Agile practices was in dire shape. It was discovered that the CEO and CFO had fraudulently created sales to boost the company's stock price. The company was being investigated by the Securities and Exchange Commission (SEC) for fraud. They had laid off more than 50% of their staff and needed to retain the rest. The executive team was focused on keeping the company afloat so they couldn't micromanage the day-to-day operations. They moved to Agile practices to give better insight into the work being done across the globe and to push ownership down to the ranks, because, quite frankly, they didn't have enough executive management remaining to oversee everything. We were surprised when the teams became focused on creating value, as they were happy and enjoyed their jobs more. The boost to morale was amazing and we can only attribute that to the new way they were working with each other.

The company ended up coming out of bankruptcy successfully, and retained more than 90% of their customers.

Framework

Transforming people, as we have seen, is largely an empowering activity for them after they get through the change curve. However, giving people a new compass for how work is done and then turning them loose is a recipe for disaster. Each team will interpret that compass differently and act accordingly. Providing the newly transformed people with a framework for success solves this problem.

The definition of a *frame* is an essential supporting structure. Create a framework for how you want to do business. Keep it lightweight. Make sure every part of it is needed by the business. Remove all processes that are done solely for the sake of doing process and remember that roles don't have to be the same as job titles. Map the skill sets for your organization to the work that needs to be done. Once a framework is learned, future change is faster.

You need to have abstraction of the processes that exist in an organization; we don't want to blow up or throw away everything, but want to streamline the processes in such a way that allows us to take advantage of the good things that already exist while fixing the things that no longer make sense.

Framework for Crossing the Chasm

Earlier we saw that most companies have a huge chasm between their strategic plans and their execution teams. We also learned that most companies don't have a good way to bridge this chasm; many just give the work to their product management or program management staff and hope for the best. Let's look at one method for crossing that chasm.

The chasm exists because we have annual plans (with each item being approximately 9–12 months of work). These are the goals that come out of our annual planning processes or our strategic planning. We expect someone in the organization to be able to take those long-term plans and break them down into chunks that can be done within two weeks. This is a monumental task and very difficult to get right. There are proven ways to go about this, however. We can take the 9- to 12-month plans and break them into three-month chunks. Even on the surface, this seems like a much more reasonable thing to do with a strategy. I can take a 12-month initiative and break that down into four three-month chunks. Then I can break down the three-month chunks into features that align to the initiative. I create a backlog of work that can be done in a three-month time frame (see Figure 5-3).

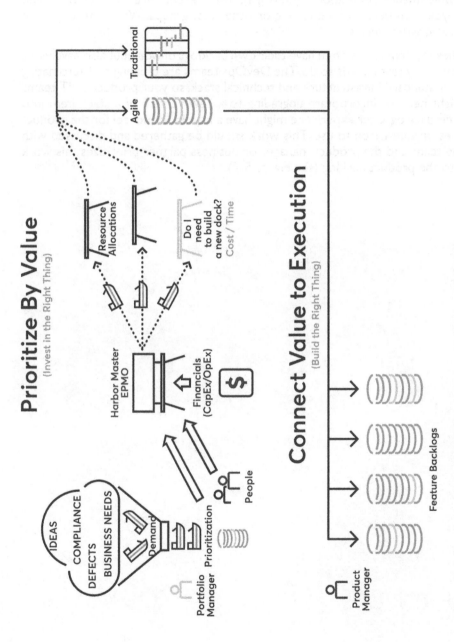

Figure 5-3. Decomposing huge initiatives into managable, estimatable features

Next, let's bring in those groups that need to give input into our work, but whose work doesn't fit into the standard sprints. These are groups like developmental operations (DevOps), user experience, architecture, and maybe even performance testing or other test groups. We like to call these people *system teams*.

These system teams often have their own backlogs of work, but also have work that every team needs to do. The DevOps teams are creating and automating your standard infrastructure and technical stack, so your product or IT teams might need to incorporate upgrading to a new version of a stack item into their backlog. User experience might have a new look and feel for the product lines or a new icon to use. This work should be gathered and discussed with the team, and the product manager or business partner prioritizes this work into the product backlog (see Figure 5-4).

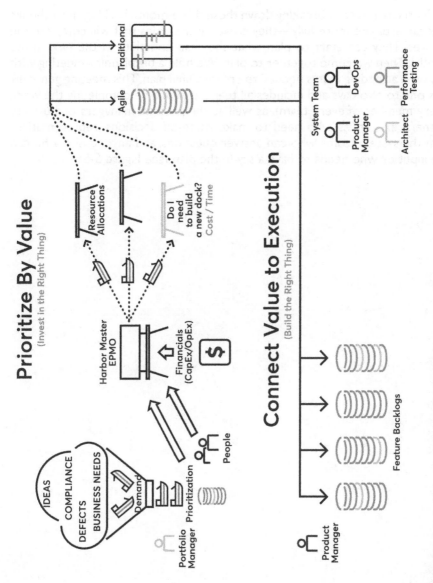

Figure 5-4. Managing dependencies and skill constraints

Now we need a way to bring this information into the execution teams so they can understand what we are asking them to do. We have initial sizing meetings to start gathering really high-level estimations—knowing these will change.

We let the teams start breaking down these three-month backlogs into chunks they can estimate more fully—they create user stories that will complete the features. They can start to plan what they can complete in the next three months. Then we come together to plan. We hold a big planning meeting with everyone attending that is needed to create a final plan. This meeting generally lasts one to two days and includes all teams that will be completing the work (every member of every team), as well as the product managers or business partners, executives who need to make trade-off decisions, representatives from the system teams who can answer questions, and anyone else who can give input or who needs to have a say in the plan (see Figure 5-5).

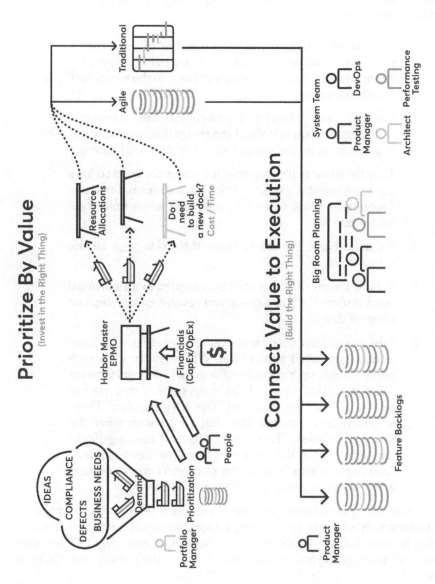

Figure 5-5. A commonsense approach to connecting strategy and execution

Although this meeting might seem expensive, it ends up being 1% to 2% of the budget for that plan. What you get for that money, though, is worth much more.

What actually happens in big room planning? There is actually a very specific agenda for the meeting:

1. *Establish why*: Have an executive member of the business team talk about why the items that are being created are important and the impact they will have on the customers and the company.

2. *Establish how*: Have a member of the enterprise architecture team talk about the things that have been put in place to assist the teams with what they are building.

3. *Allow the teams to plan together:* It's not uncommon to have the team members walking from team to team discussing dependencies and when they will need items from their fellow teams.

4. *Readouts*: Have the teams share their plan with all the other teams.

5. If there are any risks that can't be mitigated by an individual team, discuss them as a group and resolve, own, accept, or mitigate them.

6. *Take a confidence vote*: Have everyone present vote using a technique called a fist of five. When told to vote, each person holds up a number of fingers. Five fingers means "This is a great plan and I'm in agreement that we can deliver it." Four fingers means "This is a good plan." Three fingers means "I'm not sure but I'll go with what the majority believes." Two fingers means "I have significant concerns about the plan that need to be discussed." One finger means "I know the plan won't work and have information to share with the teams as to why."

Big room planning establishes a culture of alignment (everyone plans together and understands why they are working on specific items), autonomy (decision making is pushed down to the teams to determine how they will get work done), and trust (everyone is transparent about their plans and ability to deliver).

At the end of this meeting you have a full capacity plan for all teams working on the features in that three-month plan. Dependencies are mapped between teams and work. Risks are resolved, documented, mitigated, or owned (we use the ROAM method), and trade-off decisions are made when work doesn't fit (because the executives that need to make those decisions are in the room). All work that is requested or required by the systems teams is understood and part of the capacity plans that are created. In other words, you have a full release plan finalized in one or two days. In our past experience, getting to this level of agreement and sign-off took weeks of phone calls, online meetings, and hundreds of e-mails. Often, dependencies were missed—something that rarely occurs when teams are in the same room planning with each other.

Still think this meeting is expensive? How much does it cost when a dependency is found late in the development cycle? How much does it cost when a risk is actualized but wasn't planned? The cost of delay for a release is generally much more than 1% to 2% of the budget.

Simple Framework for Scaling Agile Concepts

In some organizations, after determining the strategy or portfolio direction, they hand the approved plans to the product management team to deal with. They expect those individuals will be able to somehow ensure the teams execute the plan well enough to gain the revenue and cost savings for the year. It is up to the skill set of those few individuals, and the teams they work with, to translate the goals into executable work—often without a well-defined process to do so.

Our product life cycles are supposed to take care of this, but all they have are templates for design, usability storyboards, and technical requirements. There is no accounting for the value being created, nor are the teams ever asked to keep the *value* to the customer in mind when creating the products. We often miss "why" we are asking our development teams to create the new features.

Another interesting piece to this puzzle is that many companies don't hire product management professionals for these roles. They pull people from sales, marketing, or other areas and expect them to be able to fill this strategic role. Many companies don't even realize this is what they are asking their product managers to do because they have never examined their processes to ensure they can get the expected outcomes.

So we create a strategy, base our revenue goals and operational expense reduction projects on data that aren't sound, pass off these goals to people who are not properly trained for their role, never tie the results to customer value, and wonder why our products are not selling well enough to achieve our strategic goals. In reality, it's an amazing feat if we ever meet the goals.

Pulling together all the information we've been discussing, let's take a look at how we fully tie our strategies to execution (see Figure 5-6).

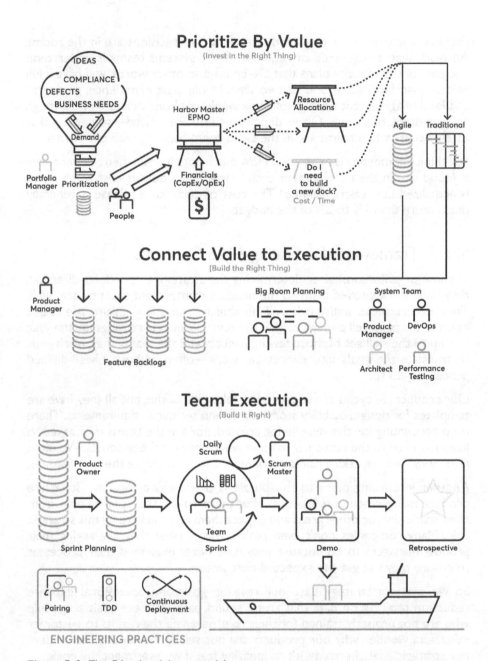

Figure 5-6. The CA value delivery model

Most of the problems we solve using Lean or Agile are really solved using common sense. We have identified this giant hole in the middle of most organizations. What if we solved it using common sense by just letting the people who are involved in the creation of the desired value talk to each other? It can't really be that simple, right? Well, consider this.

What if we bring the developers, testers, project managers, business people, finance people, infrastructure people, customer support people, and others who care about the particular thing that is being created together to discuss why this value is necessary, how they would build it, who depends on whom, the risks that need to be addressed, and how they will know they are done? Sound crazy? It's how companies—from startups to the *Fortune 50*—are solving the issue of strategy and execution not being connected.

There are lots of ways to get there—commercial frameworks, homegrown frameworks, and tools—and as we've already discussed, adoption of a specific framework isn't the answer. The idea of a framework that is focused on the creation of value and allowing for innovation is.

Platform

Do you sell products? Do your development teams and IT teams create anything that is really valuable to the company? Then why don't you need to know the real status of this value? So many companies tell us that they let their engineering and IT teams choose their tools. For certain parts of development, this is okay. For the data you need to run the business, it's not. It's no more logical to let teams use a multitude of tools for project management than it is for your finance team, your sales teams, or your customer support teams to choose their own tools.

The data you can get from Agile projects are vital to your business. Don't let anyone tell you otherwise. Let us tell you the story of two companies: one with consistent data and one that let teams choose.

We were meeting with an engineering leader who told us their team was fine with the tools they had and didn't want to discuss standardization. During the conversation, the leader mentioned that they had just been beaten to market by a competitor. This competitor had created a simple widget, one they themselves could have easily created, and patented it. They had to pay the competitor millions of dollars to use this new widget.

Well, it just so happened that we had worked with this competitor and knew exactly how they operated. They had standard practices; for example, each development team had to break down stories to no more than three days of work. The stories had to include acceptance criteria (this is how someone knows that particular story is done), estimates, and specific formatting (As A, I want, So that). They had a standard definition of done, across all teams, so when a team moved a story to accepted status, everyone, including the CTO, knew what that meant. These are pretty basic and standard parts of Scrum, but you would be surprised at how many companies don't implement standards.

This company that beat them to market had standards across all 30+ product lines. Teams worked to the same best practices and workflows; outside of those standard processes and practices, teams could do as they pleased. This company required a core set of fields that all teams used for stories, defects, test cases, and test run results, along with the consistent workflows, so they could get consistent metrics across all 30+ product lines. For example, there were seven fields in a story that were required and six in a defect that were used to create standard dashboards. Teams could add custom fields or use the remaining fields as they wanted. We had the best of both worlds: standard data to run the business and yet the teams had autonomy outside of the standards.

During our time with this company, the CTO had someone bring him an idea for a market disruptor—the same widget that our current customer was lamenting. Because the CTO knew the exact status of their projects and who was working on what, the company could create this new widget without affecting their current strategy. They beat everyone else to market with a new and patented widget, and caused all their competition to pay them millions to use it.

When it was pointed out to the current customer that the other customer had the data they needed to steer their organization more fully, without affecting current strategies, the engineering leader realized he was not fine with letting his teams use different tools and that he needed consistent data to keep up with his competition.

What will it take for you to realize that this is also what you need to run your business in today's markets? Will you need to lose so dramatically to a competitor?

An Aside About Value

As we said earlier in the book, creating value is the goal of modern business management. For the purposes of this book, value is defined as making or saving money for yourself or your company. We believe that prioritization by value—that is, the determination of what work makes or saves the **most** money at this specific moment in time—is one of the foundational principles in the adoption of modern business management. Simply put, value is creating the right thing at the right time.

It's important that you have a way to measure value that is consistent across your entire portfolio. As you plan your projects, you want to make sure you are funding and focusing on the projects that will benefit you most. You want to be able to compare each new opportunity and determine where that opportunity falls in your prioritization hierarchy.

Many companies prioritize work by grouping items into categories such as must haves, nice to haves, and should haves, or high, medium, and low. Although these groupings can help, they don't give you a real understanding of the value you are creating, nor do they give those working on the projects an understanding of which to do first.

Prioritizations should be done in a stack-rank method, meaning there is one #1, one #2, one #3, and so on. No two items should have the same rank.

There are many ways to define value to your organization and ways in which you can prioritize ideas, work that must be done, infrastructure projects, and revenue-generating projects. If you have a method defined that works for your organization, stick with that but, as always, keep your eyes open for ways to improve it.

Some companies use weighted shortest job first (WSJF), which applies value to a job based on the weight and how long the job will take. It helps you prioritize jobs that are most valuable that take the shortest time to complete first. This method can work if you don't have regulatory requirements, which often are low value to customers and can take a lot of time. They need to be prioritized to the top, but they often aren't considered valuable by customers, unless you don't meet them. The lack of meeting requirements can affect you negatively quite a bit, but meeting requirements is expected by the customers and isn't something they are usually willing to pay more for.

$$Cost\ of\ Delay = User - Business\ Value + Time\ Criticality$$
$$+ Risk\ Reduction\ and\ /\ or\ Opportunity\ Enagement$$

If you don't have a way to determine value, we recommend devising a series of questions, which you then give a weight to, and mathematically determine a value for each piece of work that needs to be done.

Include items such as these:

- Mandatory items
  - Regulatory requirements
  - Security projects
  - Keeping up with the competition's projects (i.e., moving to SaaS-based delivery)

- Revenue-generating projects
  - Number of customer (or prospect) requests
  - Revenue to be generated
  - Market size and market saturation
- Cost-saving projects
  - Productivity gains
  - Process efficiencies
  - Dollars saved

Apply a weight to each item you list and each question you ask. For example, if you have an IT project that will save your company $2 million annually, and you have a development product that is predicted to make you $1.5 million annually, you will want to make sure the IT project is completed prior to the engineering project. Prioritization is rarely this simple, however, and often requires evaluation of multiple criteria to make the final stacked rank.

Proving Value

When we first started in product development companies, one of our first steps in creating a new product was to create a proof of concept. We did this because technology was new and we weren't sure we could create something that would work. We proved the concept to make sure it was valid.

We need to flip this concept on its head today and instead prove the value of what we are creating. Instead of creating a proof of concept, consider creating a proof of value. Ensure that someone will find enough value in what you are creating to make it worth your while. If no one will actually pay for what you are creating, the value is not there.

We were working with a company that used a Lean startup concept to bring innovative ideas to market. What they found was that they had many people who would tell them they would use a certain product if they created it. Once the product was ready to be sold, however, no one was interested in actually paying for it. Again, they created a product that no one would use.

Create a product as quickly and simply as possible and then try to sell it. Use the concept of minimum viable product and make sure someone is willing to actually pay you for it prior to spending more time and money creating the full product.

Focusing on anything other than value, whether the value is to your company or your customers, is no longer an option. We can no longer spend development dollars on fun technology that no one wants to use except your engineers. We've all read the articles that indicate that 60% to 80% of products are never used. Focusing on value, rather than technology, will allow us to create products that are used and therefore valuable to our customers and business.

Getting Out of Your Own Way

Many program management organizations are still operating under the assumption that tried and true waterfall or iterative and incremental methods are best. They haven't kept up with the vast amount of research that has been done on estimation in the past few decades, and they insist on detailed up-front plans.

One of our favorite tenets of agility is maximizing the amount of work not done. Think of the countless hours your architects and principal developers have spent writing requirements, specifications, and plans for things that were never completed.

We have been creating business processes for years now. Whenever we have an executive team that will not move away from waterfall planning, we ask them one simple question: How many of you have ever had a product delivered exactly as it was planned and promised at the Phase 2 gate? This means the exact features and functionality, the exact number of resources, with high quality, and delivered on the exact date. We have never had anyone raise a hand. Essentially, none of these plans come to fruition, but we kid ourselves each time we sit in these planning gate meetings and listen to people promise us that they are 95% positive they can deliver the plan they have put forth.

If it takes a team of high-level product managers, engineers, QA personnel, technical publications staff, architects, usability experts, and so on, at least a month to create the plans for the next release (that is low compared to the three months it took when I used to create waterfall plans), then these are extremely expensive plans. If a percentage of this work is never done because it is replaced by higher priority items later in the release cycle, or because estimations were off and not as much can be completed, then you are throwing away the thousands of dollars spent on planning every release.

Stop kidding yourself in meetings where people are promising you things you know will not happen, and stop doing work you know you will throw out every year. Create a product life cycle that gives you insight and oversight for projects and doesn't require unusable plans and unnecessary work.

Streamlined Product Life Cycle

We have worked with a lot of companies that are regulated and need to pass audits and require some sort of product life cycle. Likewise, there are some companies that just like having an overarching process by which their products are made. If you work in one of these companies, this is a great place to start streamlining and removing work for work's sake.

By definition, a product life cycle has templates and phases, milestones and gates, and required steps. Start by reviewing your process and seeing what is required. We generally eliminate everything that doesn't meet the following criteria:

- It's required by an auditor or regulatory group.
- Some people need the information to do their jobs.
- We, as an organization, need this to see what is going on and how we are moving toward our goals and strategies.

Regulatory Information

Many people think things are required by a regulatory group, but in actuality it's just how things were always done within the company. Take a fresh look at anything you believe is required by regulations. Make sure you have interpreted the regulatory information correctly and ask the auditors if there is a new way others are meeting the regulations.

We were recently talking to an engineering VP who asked how we got around creating technical specification to pass the capitalization audits. I told him I have never heard of a technical specification being required for capitalization. He was told by his financial organization, though, that it was required. After further digging, we discovered that the corporate policy was written in a period when every project that could be capitalized had a detailed technical specification, so this was an easy way to prove the need for a new product vs. enhancing an existing one. The auditors weren't requiring the spec, the internal processes were. We determined three or four other things that the engineering team still needed today, which could also be used to indicate whether code was for a new product or an enhancement, and negotiated with the financial team to get their internal policies updated. Across this large organization, we saved approximately 5,000 hours of wasted work per year in teams no longer creating technical specifications that were not truly needed.

Information Others Need to Do Their Jobs

If people need a piece of information to do their jobs, you cannot remove it from the process. You can, however, change the format or ensure the knowledge is passed on in new ways.

For example, we had QA teams who told us they required a specification document so they could write test cases and ensure test coverage was at their required levels. If you use test-driven development (TDD) techniques, this information is discussed between the developers and QA engineers so you no longer need the specification. TDD is a complex topic, and we could write an entire book on how to implement it. In truth, there are already several great books that cover this topic. Although it is difficult for teams initially, there is no better way of improving the quality of the code your teams produce. Swapping out less reliable methods for new ones is imperative as you drive toward full business agility.

Information You Need

Certain pieces of information are needed by leadership so they can run the organization. For example, some form of release plan is generally needed so you know what you are getting for your investment. Data that show the real status of each chunk of work and let you see where every development dollar is going are needed to stay competitive. Data that you need to run your business should be a natural outcome of the process. Don't let anyone tell you that Agile means not writing things down, no release dates, no estimations or plans, and no status. It's simply not true.

Phases

Life cycles usually have four to five phases and they generally align to this framework:

- *Market validation*: Proving there is a market to capture and that there are buyers in the world that have a similar problem, which you can solve.

- *Planning*: Determine if and how you can create value for the company and your customers (internal or external) in response to the information found in the first phase. This usually includes capacity plans, dependencies, risks, and trade-off decisions (in and out plans).

- *Development*: Building the product that fits the needs and that provides the value.

- *Delivery*: Making sure the company, market, and product are all ready for release. This includes the official release of the product into the market.

- *Postrelease*: Anything done after the date the product is available to the market. These activities include maintenance, tracking how the product is doing in the market, and validating the data we used in the first phase to plan our work.

Most companies have a process like this today. What you need to do is evaluate every item in your process and determine if it is still valid and needed. Are there better ways to accomplish the same goals?

- Having discussions over documents thrown over a wall

- Evolving design over comprehensive specifications

- Completed products over plans

- Knowing that change will happen and planning for it rather than forcing teams to stick to a plan (complex and heavy change control processes)

Your goals should be the same goals as you are looking to get with business agility: faster time to market, better quality, higher productivity, and more engaged employees. Eliminate any process for process's sake.

So What Should Be in the Process?

Auditors like to see things written down and they want proof that what you say you will do is actually being done by the teams. In our years of streamlining process, we found there are some pieces of a life cycle that fit these models and those that you cannot easily remove.

There are three key areas that are common across regulations:

- *Documentation:* Templates, processes, and policies

- *Governance:* Verification that process is followed

- *Change management:* Proof that teams cannot change plans haphazardly

Documentation

There are some pieces of information that make sense to have written down. To determine what those pieces are, I watched what people printed and read. If leaders were printing the documents to review, the information needed to be in an easily readable document, not a presentation. The following items generally work well in documents:

- *Market analysis outcomes:* This is sometimes called a market requirements document (MRD). It explains the market or industry in general that you want to capture.

- *Business case:* Many companies wrap this into their MRD or substitute it for their MRD. It includes the numbers behind the request. Examples include market sizing, available market, current market penetration, revenue projections for a new product, and so on.

- *Go to market plan*: This includes the channels to enable, new markets to conquer, how you want your company and products to be perceived in the market, differentiators, and so on.

- *Release plans*: These cover what is planned in the release, benefits of the new features, windows of opportunity (including cost of delay), and who is involved. You can also include future plans such as the internationalization schedule, infrastructure updates, and accessibility alignment.

- *Master quality plan*: This is created at the start of a project. It's the overall quality plan, and details how you ensure quality will be built into the system. It includes all types of testing, who will test, security and open source scans, if any parts will not be tested, metrics to be used to show release readiness, and quality release criteria.

- *Release package*: Created throughout and at the end of the release, it details the major points and changes that occurred. In regulated environments, it can be used instead of going back and updating planning documents. The release package includes information about the entire release. Some companies don't create these, but we have found that they are invaluable when you need to remember what happened during a release from a previous year. The information should cover the entire project, including requirements planned vs. completed, and record any major changes to the projects.

If you are audited, there are also a few other documents that are generally required:

- *Quality process*: This is the general, corporate process you use to ensure quality is planned in, and then verified. It includes who does what and when. For example, your process might start with someone in QA reading the MRD; reviewing requirements as they are broken down into initiatives, features, and stories; then the types of testing done during the iteration, postiteration, performance testing, and security scans; and so on. Include who does each step and how you ensure integrity of environments and systems in accordance with your regulations.

- *Test reports:* These are the response to the master quality plan. It's completed at the end of the project and details what happened during the release, documenting that all planned tests were completed. Include final release metrics. :

Governance

In waterfall processes, gates are heavy and they are meant to keep people from passing until they can gain approval. As your teams begin to release products more frequently, gates can slow them down, especially if the leadership needed to sign off on those gates are busy.

In Agile methods, we documented gates as milestones that were a natural outcome of the process. They are like an arch that must be passed under, allowing teams to continue unless they are told to stop. I also aligned the milestones to meetings that already occurred. If you are doing the planning meetings detailed earlier in this chapter, that can also serve as your Phase 2 milestone. Leadership is in the meeting, hearing the readouts of the teams, and participating in trade-off discussions, so there shouldn't need to be any additional approval.

Traceability is another piece to governance. It means being able to track a requirement from idea to release, including all defects, tests, and test runs.

- Portfolio items should be detailed.

- Story descriptions must be complete, including acceptance criteria.

- Show good test case coverage.

- All tests run and passed and defects are captured.

- All changes are tracked, including who did them and when.

Your processes should naturally include full traceability and your tools should be able to support it easily and consistently.

Change Management

In most companies we visit, change management is synonymous with control. It is a method used to control what the teams can change about the detailed plans they wrote many months ago. In reality, our world is changing much too quickly for these antiquated processes to work well. We need to plan for change rather than see it as something to avoid. Many change management processes keep your company from succeeding.

So when do you need change management? Is it whenever any small change occurs? Are there only certain types of changes that really matter? In working with many customers, we found there are a few times when change management is needed:

1. When regulations require it.

2. When a promise is changed. This can be a promise to an executive, to a customer, or to another team. All three of these scenarios require some process around how to handle these types of changes and who needs to know about the change.

Create a process that alerts the appropriate individuals whenever a change to a promise is made. Require silos to come down, by forcing conversations if a team made a promise to another team that they can no longer meet. If approval is needed for certain promise changes, add that to the process. We found that in most cases, a meeting is needed to discuss the change and agree on mitigations more than it is to gain approval.

If your process requires it, you will need to update documents as things change. Depending on your regulations, you may need to update a plan document. If regulations do not have specific requirements for how a change is documented, you may be able to simply update the Release Package to note the change and the decisions made. Your planning documents stay baselined to the original plan.

Creating a streamlined life cycle

If we look at the diagram of the CA value delivery model shown in Figure 5-6, we can see where the process defines itself.

Market Validation

Before we plan our portfolio, we do market analysis and determine a go-to-market plan. We ensure we have the right number of teams to do the work and we create budgets. The meetings you hold to determine the portfolio plan are the first milestone in your process—we called this the market validation milestone (see Figure 5-7).

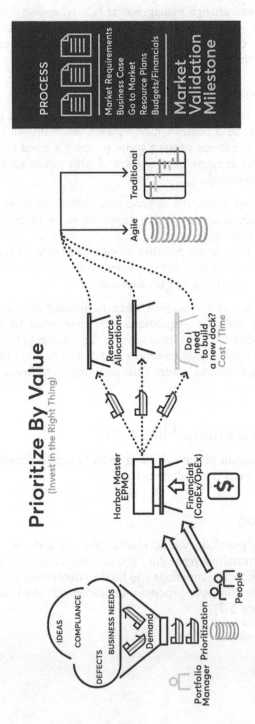

Figure 5-7. Phase 1: Market validation

Planning

Then we move into quarterly planning. This takes the place of release planning. During this time, planning for the upcoming quarterly release is completed. Depending on your regulatory requirements, you will need more or fewer documents during this time.

System teams give input to ensure all work that is needed to be done by the teams is included in the backlog, and therefore, release plan (see Figure 5-8).

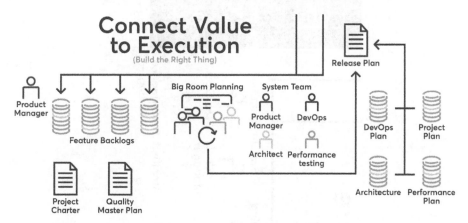

Figure 5-8. Big room planning is the planning milestone

We recommend a project charter document that includes information on features and benefit statements for the upcoming release, information on things like accessibility plans, internationalization, infrastructure, and architectural information. These are things that often take longer than one release to complete. Include information about usability, architectural upgrades, operations information, and any other system teams.

If you need master quality plans, do them now as well. We found a master quality plan (described earlier in this chapter) fulfills this regulation for many agencies. As you move toward continuous delivery, your master quality plans might remain relatively static. Review your requirements around quality plans because you might be able to create one to have on file and only update it if you change how you do your various types of testing.

The release plan is a natural outcome of the big room planning. We're betting you already write down somewhere what decisions were made during the planning meeting, what was agreed on, what is in scope and out of scope, the dependencies, and the risks. You have a capacity plan, so you know the plan is solid.

That's it. That's the natural outcome of the big room planning and it is perfect for filling in an official release plan (see Figure 5-9).

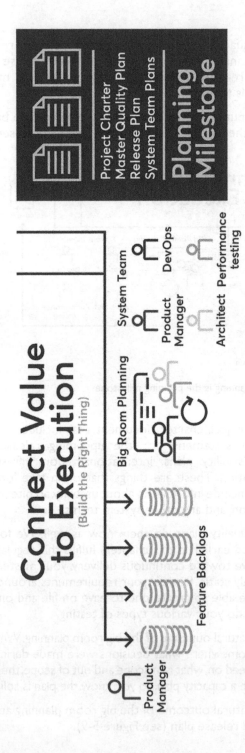

Figure 5-9. Phase 2: Planning

Gate/Milestone

The milestone is the big room planning event. It's where the final plan for the quarter is set and final decisions are made. Dependencies are mapped, trade-off decisions are made, risks are mitigated or owned, and capacity plans are set. This is not to say that the decisions cannot change during the quarter, but generally, the plan is set. Teams have an executable plan they can begin working on and the business has something that they can use to track against as they create value for the customers.

Development

Generally, there aren't any documents to create while the product is being developed, unless you have some required by regulations. Document the process the teams use to create the products. This includes final grooming of the backlog, iteration planning meetings, standup meetings, definition of done, story acceptance process, iteration review meetings (demos), definition of potentially shippable code, and retrospectives.

Define this phase at a high level, but include details where necessary to ensure discipline and quality are driven into the process. The best process we created was documented on an internal web site and the development phase was described in about six paragraphs. Remember, the more you document the more the teams need to follow. Therefore, unless it's regulated or needed for you to get consistent data to run and steer your business, leave it out.

The main thing to note are the ceremonies that accompany iteration planning, the demo and iteration review, and the retrospective, because this is where the majority of collaboration occurs and where decisions are made (see Figure 5-10).

Team Execution
(Build it Right)

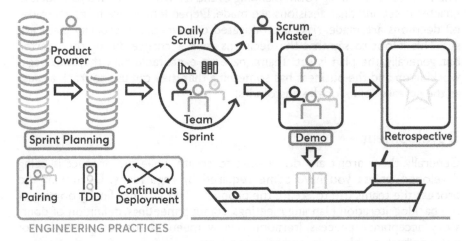

Figure 5-10. Phase 3: Development

Testing is also done during development and should be part of standard iterations. If you need to do additional testing after all functionality is complete (for things like security scanning, performance, etc.), you can document this in your process as well.

Delivery

Delivery is when you release your product into the market. Many companies call this general availability (GA). Depending on the type of release you are doing, this can be a major impact to your company for a full-blown, major, on-premises release, or it can be a fully automated, quick update if you continuously deliver into a cloud or SaaS environment.

You still need to make sure your company, the market, and your product are all ready for the release. Also include final release criteria, metrics, and any tasks that need to be done to complete all regulatory requirements prior to releasing in the market.

Postrelease

Document the work you do to ensure your product is operating in live environments as you intended. You could gather certain support metrics, defect leakage, top ten call drivers, and sales numbers.

If you had business cases you used to determine market sizing, projected revenue numbers for new products, and so on, be sure to track how valid these numbers and predictions were. Many companies fail to validate these numbers and never use a continuous improvement process for the data they use to make their investment bets. The companies that do this well almost always see gains in market share, but also in nontangible metrics like net promoter scores (NPS), customer satisfaction (CSAT), and customer experience (CX) scoring. If clients don't validate these metrics, they look at why their sales teams aren't selling or why marketing doesn't work. Although these things also play a part in a product's success, we found that more likely the numbers you used to base your initial decision were not correct.

Pulling It All Together

Looking at all the components just mentioned, the flow of work and process looks like Figure 5-11.

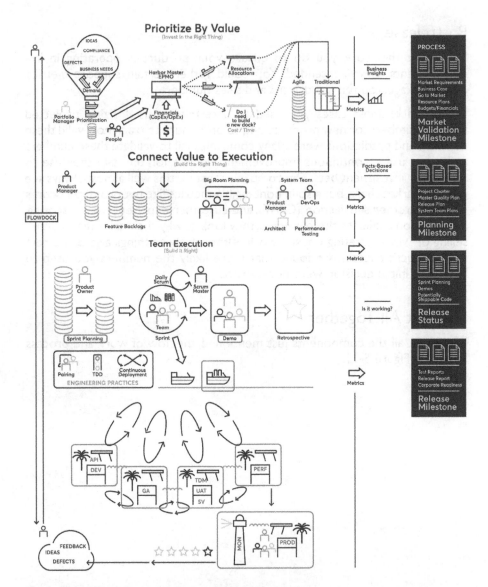

Figure 5-11. Four-phase process over Agile methodologies

In Figure 5-10 where we discussed Agile ceremonies, we represented shipping value as a huge cargo ship with a single increment of value on board. No shipping company would actually send a cargo ship out with only one box on it, though. They fill up the ship. Too often we see clients do this as well: They take the potential value that is created by each iteration or sprint and wait until they have a whole shipload of value before actually shipping it out so their customers can use it. A much better (and Agile) model would be to replace the huge ship with speedboats. Each speedboat can hold only a small amount of value, but many of them together can be moving the potential value between your various development environments, and eventually into the customers' environments. The key is to put the things you build in the hands of your customers as quickly as is practical. Potential value that is created by a team is really not all that useful. It only becomes "real" when the users for whom you created it can use it.

When you take all of the process information and create a product lIfe cycle that auditors like, it looks like Figure 5-12.

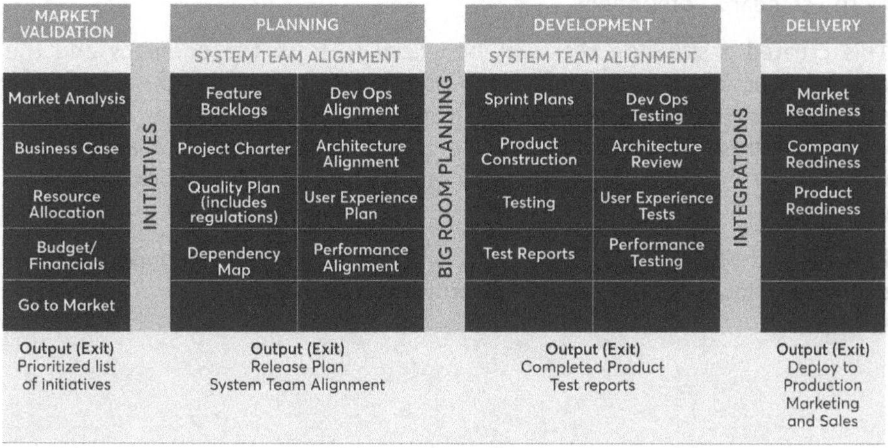

MARKET VALIDATION		PLANNING				DEVELOPMENT			DELIVERY
		SYSTEM TEAM ALIGNMENT				SYSTEM TEAM ALIGNMENT			
Market Analysis	INITIATIVES	Feature Backlogs	Dev Ops Alignment	BIG ROOM PLANNING		Sprint Plans	Dev Ops Testing	INTEGRATIONS	Market Readiness
Business Case		Project Charter	Architecture Alignment			Product Construction	Architecture Review		Company Readiness
Resource Allocation		Quality Plan (includes regulations)	User Experience Plan			Testing	User Experience Tests		Product Readiness
Budget/ Financials		Dependency Map	Performance Alignment			Test Reports	Performance Testing		
Go to Market									
Output (Exit) Prioritized list of initiatives		Output (Exit) Release Plan System Team Alignment				Output (Exit) Completed Product Test reports			Output (Exit) Deploy to Production Marketing and Sales

Figure 5-12. Standard four-phase product life cycle

Your life cycle might have additional required regulatory documents. Add in what is needed, after you have reviewed your latest regulations. Make sure you are interpreting them in the most efficient way.

Streamline Regulatory Requirements

When you have to meet regulatory requirements, ensure your teams are enabled as much as possible. Requiring each development team to read, understand, and interpret regulations is a productivity killer and puts your organization at risk. Create tools and templates to help them implement and adhere to the regulations as easily as possible.

At one company, we worked with the chief information security officer (CISO) to understand the PCI regulations and determine how they impacted our products. Then we created a checklist that the teams used to ensure the software complied. We grouped regulations where possible so teams could meet the requirements more easily.

We then reviewed the standard infrastructure that was being used and found that when components were used as designed by our DevOps team, a large portion of the requirements were met. For example, using our DevOps' standard single-sign-on component met 15 line items on the spreadsheet.

We therefore added a column to the spreadsheet for the single-sign-on standard. If teams designed their product to these standards, they could filter the spreadsheet and make 15 of the requirements on their list disappear. In other words, if a team used our single-sign-on component fully as designed, they could remove all the requirements from the checklist that were covered by the standard component.

This created a situation that was beneficial to both the company and the development teams. It encouraged our teams to follow the corporate standards to reduce the number of regulatory requirements they had to deal with, and it freed up the teams' time to do more valuable work. It encouraged usage of our certified components by making teams do less work when they used them.

Make sure those responsible for your processes include these types of time-saving techniques to fulfill your regulatory requirements.

Introducing the Modern Business

The modern business, focuses on bringing Agile principles and practices through the entire organization. This means optimizing the whole, rather than incenting one group to optimize at the expense of another. In the end, becoming a modern business is really about creating an environment of alignment, autonomy, and trust. That sounds simple, but it's very difficult. However, if you can get your teams and the business to align on what's important, push decision making to the teams within your organization, and as we discussed earlier, establish collaboration based on trust, you are on the right path to becoming a modern business.

When talking to companies about bringing agility into their entire organization, we generally start with Lean practices to do so. Some of the main practices are shown in the House of Lean.

House of Lean

The House of Lean is a model created to explain the fundamental Lean principles. It has been taken and modified by many organizations to suit their styles. We have recently seen houses that have anywhere from two to four pillars, but the one we like best, and the one that seems to adhere to the Lean fundamentals the most, looks like Figure 6-1, from the Lean Systems Society.

© CA 2018
D. Dockery and L. Knudsen, *Modern Business Management*,
https://doi.org/10.1007/978-1-4842-3261-3_6

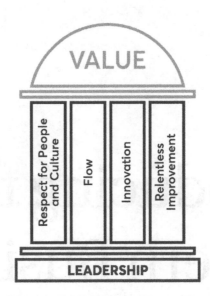

Figure 6-1. House of Lean

Value

Lean starts with value. Everything should be tied to customer value. When studied, customers are only interested in the value they are receiving. They don't care whether other customers are perceiving value, nor does it matter if the customer is external or internal. Customers tend to care only about the value they, themselves, are receiving.

Every action we do within our organizations should bring value to someone, either the customer or the business. This is the "roof" that all other Lean principles support.

Respect for People and Culture

Respect for people and culture is a fundamental trait of Lean. It is believed that people can thrive and be extremely smart when given the chance and the right environment. Strive to understand everyone in your organization and allow the personalities of the team members to thrive as they fulfill responsibilities, reach their potential, and continue to improve.

People tend to behave and grow to meet our expectations of them. If we expect greatness, they strive to be great. If we expect mediocrity, they become mediocre. It's a self-fulfilling prophecy. Expect your employees to continue to improve, give them the autonomy to flourish, and allow them to think of new and better ways of working.

Flow

Lean flow is about how work moves through your organization. Whether it's written down and agreed on or haphazard, every bit of work that is being done by your organization flows from one step to another until it is complete (or until someone stops asking about it). In other words, there is a process for each item of work being done in your organization.

Throughput is about measuring the number of items that move through a process or system. It measures how much work can be completed, or how quickly work flows through your processes.

When we talk about optimizing flow, we look at the entire process through which a piece of work moves and we ensure the whole process is optimized. You want all of your most frequently used processes to be as efficient as possible. One technique to optimize flow is value stream mapping. We'll look at flow optimization, especially as it pertains to incenting employees, in a bit. The main point to take away is that you need to optimize an entire flow, not just a piece.

Innovation

If you read five articles on Lean innovation you will read five different definitions of it. The most discussed definition is about getting the most streamlined and wanted product to market as quickly as possible. This means that knowing what your customers really want, and letting them give feedback as you are creating it, will result in the best innovation. Being innovative in a Lean sense does not mean needing some big bang jump. Innovation can be removing waste from a process and creating the best product to meet your customers' desires.

Relentless Improvement

Relentless means "unrelenting; unyielding" according to *Webster's Unabridged Dictionary*.[1] We have all been told we need to have continuous improvement, but Lean takes it to another level. Every day everyone in the organization should look at what they are doing and determine how to be more efficient and effective. They are to incessantly advance what they are doing to the most optimal point.

Think of how powerful your organization could be if every person in it did this for just one week. The improvements to your company would most likely be vast and dramatic. As a leader of your organization, your job is to get every employee to this point: to constantly strive to improve.

---

[1] *Webster's Unabridged Dictionary* (Springfield, MA: G. C. Merriam, 1913).

Leadership

If you look at the House of Lean shown in Figure 6-1, leadership is the foundation on which all other pillars sit. You must have good solid leadership who understand how to create an environment in which all the other principles can thrive. Ensuring your leaders allow the teams to be self-organizing, while still providing the guidance and mentoring each member needs, is key.

Lean leaders are coaching and mentoring rather than managing metrics and reading reports. That's not to say data aren't important; they are vital to being able to run and steer your business. People aren't managed by data, though; work is.

Bringing Lean and Agile Practices Into Your Entire Organization

We have found that in our experience companies follow a similar path when transforming (Figure 6-2).

1. First to transform are generally IT and technology teams.

2. Next are how work is planned at the program level and deployment, including continuous integration.

3. Then comes portfolio-level planning and continuous delivery.

4. Finally we see agility move into the entire organization, including ideation through business management.

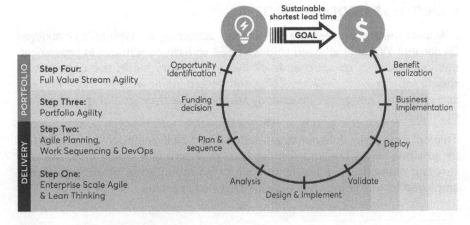

Figure 6-2. Phases of Agile adoption

Companies start transformations and then hit a tipping point where the need for the next level of agility arises. Based on our experience in the last 15 years of coaching leaders in large enterprises, transformation generally takes about three years of continuous improvement.

We have worked with many companies as they move through their transformation. Especially in years past, companies started with all the teams that create products and many IT teams: those that keep the lights on as well as those running projects to manage new infrastructure. As these teams become more agile, and start to deliver value on a more regular basis, there becomes a need to feed new work to these teams at a more frequent pace, and to release products more quickly.

This is the tipping point that we see when companies look to change their planning processes and their integration processes. If your individual development teams have been using Agile methods for at least a year and you are not feeling the pressure to improve the planning and delivery processes, it's safe to say your teams are not using a disciplined approach, nor are you getting any benefits from the Agile practices. Go back to the basics and get your individual execution teams on track.

When you plan full projects and programs using a more streamlined approach, and your teams have the infrastructure and automation in place to integrate continuously, you will start to feel a need to do portfolio planning and releasing more frequently. This is the tipping point that we see when companies ask us to help them rework their portfolio planning and implement full continuous delivery. If the DevOps organization wasn't formed when continuous integration was instituted, it will be as continuous delivery is implemented.

Creating a DevOps area within your IT organization is an entire topic in and of itself. What we have seen are the general practices within IT that pertain to the support, delivery, and operations of your products go through a transformation of their own. They change the way they work, collaborate, and work with the teams they support in an effort to get completed work into customers' hands more frequently. There are many great books (and some not-so-great books) written on this subject, so we won't go into great detail here.

Releasing products more quickly will force a change for all other departments in your organization. There is often pressure to figure out how to market smaller product increments, how to sell when you don't have the next "major" release, and how to support products that are delivered to market continuously. Many companies realize that some of the financial reports they have been using no longer seem to work as throughput increases and more value is created. Old financial models show the new way of working costs more when, in fact, the reverse is true. We talk more about this and how you can change in the next chapter.

At this point, companies can feel a real reluctance from those departments outside of IT or product development who never expected to have Agile methodologies and Lean practices affect them. As those departments that create the products move faster, though, there is a need for every part of your organization to streamline processes and figure out how to bring Lean and Agile into how they do business. Let's look at some specific ways we've seen this manifest in companies.

A few years ago, we were called by a leading financial organization because they had trouble delivering their best-selling product to market: They kept finding quality issues so they delayed the release. Product management saw the additional time and added in another feature, which led to quality issues, which led to additional delays. They were caught in a very bad cycle and hadn't released for more than two years. We reworked their product life cycle and then instituted Agile practices (specifically Scrum) for the execution teams. We instituted best practices (no user story of more than three or four days of work, standardized definition of done including zero defects, standard planning practices), and implemented a standard tool to track work that had consistent data and workflows for all teams worldwide.

As the teams became proficient in these practices, we needed more frequent builds. We implemented continuous integration. We were still delivering on premises, so we had nine-month-plus release cycles, but we made sure work was clean when it was developed.

We also lightened up the planning cycles and allowed for new requriements to be given to the teams (swapping out pieces from the current plan in a 1:1 technique—so for every hour the new requirement took, something of equal length was removed from the release). We were not overworking our teams, but giving them a sustainable pace—something they hadn't had for years.

During this portion of the transformation, the company made the strategic decision to move delivery of key products to a cloud environment. We built up our DevOps, ProdOps, and ServiceOps organizations, determined our infrastructure plan for the cloud environment, and started our teams on the refactoring process so products could be delivered on the same technology stack.

This strategic and infrastructure change allowed us to deliver more frequently. As we refactored products and moved to faster delivery schedules, we broke the marketing, support, and sales departments. We didn't mean to, but we hadn't realized how delivering product every six weeks would completely break the marketing campaign strategy. No longer did we have "big bang" releases to market and sell. Our support teams didn't know how to keep up with the continuous changes being delivered. We ended up reworking all of our departments to align with the new way of working.

We also realized that how we incented our leadership was no longer working. We had MBOs set to encourage leaders to optimize their portion of the business, often at the expense of another department. The better each did at optimizing their own teams, the more bonus they received, even if that meant completely breaking down another area of the company. So we refactored our entire bonus structure.

Then we noticed that some of our financial reports no longer worked as a way to truly measure what was happening.

The remainder of this chapter talks specficially about each of these departments and how we looked to solve these issues.

Lean Accounting

For many customers that we talk to, their transformation is stuck because:

- Their financial reporting and accounting processes are at odds with the changes they are making.

    - Activity-based accounting shows the transformation is more expensive than the predictive way of doing work.

    - Activity-based accounting shows that the organization is delivering less value; for example, incremental delivery (delivering the most valuable part of a funded project and moving on to something more important) vs. large-scale delivery (delivering the entire funded project regardless of value to the company).

- Traditional accounting or activity-based accounting was designed to measure a more traditional, predictive process.

- Lean or Agile "breaks the rules" of traditional organizational metrics and established norms. For example, traditional accounting generally shows that big batches are more economical than small ones.

- Activity-based accounting is, at best, unsuited to measuring your new organization and, at worst, becomes an impediment to further transformation and is actively hostile to Lean or Agile thinking.

What if you could control, measure, and manage your financial reporting and accounting processes in a way that reflects the Lean or Agile thinking and values that you've adopted?

What Is Lean Accounting?

Lean accounting can best be understood by examining its two main objectives.

- As with any application of Lean, apply Lean principles and methods to your accounting practices, internal controls, and financial-metric gathering processes. Just like in other Lean applications, the main goal is to eliminate wasted work, reduce bottlenecks, free up capacity, and become more efficient and effective.

- Next, align your accounting processes to influence Lean change and continuous improvement. Many companies are eliminating traditional methods such as activity-based costing and transactional control systems. Also, many standard financial reports do not show reality when used on Agile and Lean practices. Instead, we want to focus on value-based pricing, the flow of the work, obstacles and bottlenecks, where we can improve flow, and the operational and financial impact of the improvements we are making.

Lean accounting clearly identifies the financial impact of Lean improvements with the primary function of understanding the impact of waste elimination and the additional capacity such improvements bring.

What Is the Value of Lean Accounting?

Lean accounting motivates long-term improvements and efficiencies across the entire organization. It brings the financial and control-oriented portions of an organization into alignment with the parts of an organization that are exploring new ways to do work and adopting Lean or Agile thinking. However, Lean accounting is not simply a "financial thing." It's a way of looking at the performance of an organization and determining the value of the work or products being produced, as opposed to simply counting the hours necessary to create services or products.

When working with companies, we have found that by reviewing the accounting, control, and measurement processes we can update their processes with a new Lean way of looking at performance that can expose even more opportunities for improvement. We can give people at all levels of the organization additional information on the real value being created by organizing the measures around value streams, keeping true to the Lean value stream management principles.

Customer value is key, and we can more easily measure true value using Lean accounting principles. Traditional cost measurements become less effective, as we show in the following example.

We were working with a company that was realizing some great benefits of agility: better predictability, faster time to market, and improved productivity. However, the practices of their finance department often showed that products were costing more to create. It became apparent that the practices of the departments other than IT and product development were not in alignment with the Agile or Lean principles.

We started with the finance group and we created Lean value stream maps of their processes. We cut out all unnecessary work or things that no longer served the company because of how we were now developing and delivering our products.

We stopped measuring costs.

Let that sink in for a minute. We convinced the finance group that it was in the company's best interest to discontinue measuring the cost of things and we started measuring spending. We determined that measuring the cost of things in hindsight (things have to cost something before you can measure what they cost) led us to rat-hole discussions about allocations. We never determined the root cause of the costs.

Instead, we started measuring the customer value we were creating. In tracing our processes within the organization we realized that our teams, when truly Agile, naturally controlled spending and costs. Because our productivity was increasing and we were releasing to the customers more frequently, we could measure customer value and as a drill-down metric, track spending. This allowed us to see the root cause of our spending in our constant pursuit of providing increased customer value at a reduced spend.

- Business decisions = spending
- Decisions can change; therefore, spending can change
- Spending changes = cost changes

We identified issues and removed root causes based on weekly reporting of spending. We used continuous improvement techniques to drive out unnecessary spending of any type. We taught every area of the business to look for waste in spending. These can be time wasters, money wasters, or producing products in which no one finds value.

We also moved away from basing the price of our products on our costs. Instead we looked at customer value and then factored in supply and demand, and what the market would bear. Our primary basis for the pricing of our products was no longer our cost, though. It was the value to the customer.

When creating software, you can create something quickly and cheaply that has a very high value to a customer who uses it. Conversely, you can spend millions on something that no one deems valuable. This becomes extremely evident when you recall the statistic that between 60% and 80% of an enterprise software product is never used.

When you focus your financial metrics on customer value instead of cost, you realize that anything you spend on a product not used is expensive to your organization. You will always spend money—your people cost you the same regardless of the value they create—but what something costs requires you to look at money spent in relation to value achieved. When you start to drive all your teams to develop only those products that provide high customer value, your value to spend ratio starts looking very positive for the bottom line.

Now let's talk about some of the other departments that need to change for your organization to achieve a modern way of doing business.

Human Resources

Earlier, we defined Lean and the practices that it supports. One of the last organizations to embrace Lean and Agile practices is often HR.

We now know that optimizing an entire process from start to finish is the path to gaining the most efficiencies for your organization. So is your HR organization still incenting leadership to optimize just their group? For example, if your bonuses and executive payouts are based on how well one leader did in comparison to another, on how efficient and effective their department or team was, then how likely will they be to focus on creating the optimal flow?

When you pit leaders against each other and incent them to optimize just one portion of a process or flow, you create bottlenecks or deficiencies in other areas. This can affect your business quite a bit if one group is negatively affecting another. Stress levels rise, morale drops, and the company suffers in lost productivity. Be sure you are *not* incenting behaviors that cause your company to be suboptimal. Incent so the company wins, not just a few leaders.

The practices, training, and tools HR implements should support the Lean and Agile practices being used in the organization. Many companies are adopting a much more shallow hierarchy and eliminating levels of middle management to bring frontline workers closer to the top-tier executives.

How transparent is your HR organization? Transparency is a key tenet of any Agile practice. Although there are always portions of data that cannot be made available to everyone, ensure your policies are not to hide information that could help employees understand how the company works, or even more important, understand why your company exists.

Another change we see within modern HR organizations is a move away from systems of record to systems of collaboration. Enabling employees of all groups and in all geographic locations to collaborate is key. Knowledge sharing and information sharing is part of every modern business.

Sales

Your sales teams need to learn how to sell product without having a large or "major" future release to sell. When you delivery continuously, or frequently, there is never a big bang release to sell. The difference is that the product is always being improved, which allows customer-requested features to potentially make it into the product at a faster rate.

Make sure your sales leaders understand how to sell products that are continuously delivered. This includes SaaS and cloud products. Moving your stack to Amazon Web Services? Don't forget to retrain your salespeople.

So how do you do this? You sell based on what exists today and you develop a solid program for hearing the voice of your customers and where they want the product to go. We generally see modern companies spend 10% to 20% of their budgets on the things their customers tell them they want. This includes both prospective customers and current customers.

If your salespeople are used to including future features in their current sales proposals, get a reign on that now. Explain to them why: You can't move to continuous delivery and meet your strategic goals if your development teams are constantly being disrupted to work on a feature only one customer wants, even if it's your latest sale and newest customer.

This is why everyone in your organization needs to understand where the markets are moving and how you want to respond. How committed are you to your current strategies vs. the features that new and potential customers want? Are you market-driven or single-sale-driven?

If your strategy is solid, and you are relying on it to meet revenue numbers, you cannot let your sales teams destroy that by selling features that don't exist. In the same light, if your salespeople are telling you that customers want something completely different than your strategy defines, make sure your strategies have solid data behind them. We're finding quite a few organizations that give their market analysts less than two weeks to review what is happening in the world and to come up with numbers and requirements based on that research. This is generally done on top of day jobs. How good do you think those data are? What if these folks could have the time they needed to get the market analysis right so you could place your strategic bets on things not only your current customers, but adjacent markets, want?

Place your bets in the best areas to accelerate your corporate growth and train your salespeople on the new techniques they need to sell in the world of continuous delivery.

We're seeing another trend in sales teams that have long sales cycles: the sprint or iteration. Sales leadership and regional teams are checking in on progress made and work completed through the sales cycles, every two weeks. These meetings mimic the sprint demos that execution teams have. Salespeople talk about the current deals they are working, share anything they have created in the past two weeks, and collaborate to solve impediments they have run into. Everyone in the region can share how they have moved past a similar sales inhibitor, and new techniques and tools are exchanged.

Sales teams are using the Agile practices that make sense to them and implementing a team approach to sales.

Marketing

In the same way that sales no longer has a major release to sell, marketing no longer has a bunch of new features and benefit statements to wrap campaigns around. Instead, marketing programs can be run at any time and are often based on market needs, solutions to problems, trade shows, and events.

Marketing teams are also beginning to work in sprints and show their work every two weeks. They are demoing new messaging and techniques with leadership and other marketing teams to get feedback and continuously improve their marketing pieces. They are using Lean startup techniques to prove out online, digital, and print campaigns before they roll them out.

Campaigns are becoming iterative, with experimentation becoming the norm before big budgets are spent. Marketers are responding more quickly to market changes and new ideas, and they are open to frequent feedback. Digital marketing allows for more frequent updates to messaging and makes it easier to keep with with disruption.

Agile marketing is now a buzz phrase and new ideas are being developed as new technologies and new social media applications are adopted. Some marketing teams even have their own technology workers, or hire outside firms to create technologically rich marketing campaigns.

Portfolio and Program Management

Many companies today have PMO offices that are just starting to look at how they need to change to continue to be effective for the company. We need to move away from the command and control centers of the traditional PMO office and apply the value that the PMO office provides in a new way.

Over the decades, PMO and EPMO offices have driven risk, cost, and issues out of the execution teams. When teams are using Agile practices, though, they should be doing this for themselves. Teams become self-organizing, and they take accountability and responsibility for the products they create and the commitments they make to the company. They provide detailed data as a natural outcome of their Agile practices. Being disciplined with your Agile practices means that your project managers no longer need to run around asking people for their status.

However, many companies lose a lot of value in their Agile practices by allowing teams to dictate how they implement agility in their organizations. Teams start telling leadership that doing Agile means no planning, no release dates, no estimating, no design, and no documentation. The list goes on, but none of this could be farther from the truth. If you are implementing agility with the goal of seeing the results promised (faster time to market, improved quality, increased productivity, better predictability, and improved morale), you need some consistent practices and consistent data and workflows, or you will not realize these results.

The PMO office should be masters at Lean and Agile practices like value stream mapping so they can help streamline all areas of the organization. They should drive efficiency and effectiveness throughout the entire organization, starting with all the processes they own. Remove all process for process's sake and make sure every template, requirement, and metric has a distinct and valuable purpose.

The PMO office should also be focusing on value and outcomes. Managing projects is being replaced by managing products and outcomes. This causes a much bigger change than the simple word change implies: It makes companies focus on a completely different aspect.

At first glance this seems like semantics, but take a step back and think about the differences. If we ask you about your projects, what would you tell us? You would probably talk about the budgets, how you prioritize, the strategy behind them, whether you have the resources to complete them, whether you are on track to complete them on time, whether you are on budget, and if the project will have the right level of quality.

Now, if I ask you about your products we will have an entirely different conversation. You will tell me about how your products improve the business of your customers, or you might give me quotes from the latest complements your customers have given you. You will tell me about the differentiators for your products vs. your competition.

The first conversation centers around what is happening inside your organization. It focuses on you and how the work is affecting your company. The second conversation is focused on things external to your company, specifically your customers and the value you are providing them. It aligns your thoughts, words, processes, and goals around value instead of around internal status.

In traditional project management you are worried about the items on the left side of Figure 6-3. As you update and Lean out your thinking and ways of doing business, you will transition to thinking about the ideas on the right side.

Legacy Mindset	Lean Thinking
• Schedule-focused	• Value-focused
• Yearly budgets	• Incremental funding
• Large upfront planning	• Continuous steering
• Track to plan	• Plan to replan
• Individual capacity	• Team capacity
• Elastic resource pool	• (mostly) Fixed capacity
• Assign FTEs to projects	• Flow features through teams
• Program = group of Projects	• Program = group of Teams
• Plan-Based	• Adaptive

Figure 6-3. Legacy vs. Lean thinking

This one change in focus has a dramatic impact on the company. It often causes companies to start focusing on funding outcomes instead of projects. It changes delivery models and how we measure success.

This is the future of the PMO office: measuring the value provided and the outcomes achieved, managing the strategy and keeping an eye on market trends to ensure the organization is not being disrupted, and managing the business instead of just the execution teams.

Just as the PMO office coached teams on how to work in a waterfall environment, they should really be the leaders in the Agile transformations within their organizations. They should align their product life cycles and SDLCs to allow for Agile practices to be used. They should understand the steps teams go through as they learn how to work agily. They should define the best practices, including the definition of done for the organization, and make sure it includes only those items that are truly important. They should define the standard metrics to be used and the workflows to be followed, so that executives have the information and data they need to run the business. How the company meets strategic directives through outcomes and value, with top quality, should be driven from the PMO office.

So what does a modern PMO office do? They apply all their skills to the entire business. In the same way that project managers drove execution against plans in the 1990s and 2000s, they need to drive strategic goals, business outcomes, and efficiencies within the entire organization today.

Strategy

Managing strategy is key for all organizations in fast-changing markets. Disruptors can launch at any time and take market share quickly. Being able to respond to new competition, respond to new market problems, and innovate new strategies quickly is vital to long-term success. PMO organizations should expand their skills to include keeping up on the market and the business responses to those market changes.

When a new idea or opportunity arises, how does your company respond? Do you know exactly how much value has been created against each current strategy and initiative? Can you tell which teams have completed the most valuable pieces of a strategy so the new work can flow to them?

There should be no need to run around asking people if they have really completed some portion of a project. The data created through disciplined Agile practices should provide this naturally. Work marked as done should meet your corporate definition of done so you know the exact status of every item of work. With the right data, steering your organization and responding to disruption, or even disrupting the market yourself, has never been easier.

Project management is no longer about driving teams to complete tasks. The teams commit to a plan and then meet those plans. Status, and the data that prove the status, are a natural outcome of good, disciplined Agile practices.

Planning

When we worked on software development teams in the 1980s and 1990s, we used to create these huge plans for everything we wanted to do. There was even a phase where we "planned to plan" and this was considered good. We thought the more you knew about what we were trying to create before we jumped in, the better the product would be.

We tried to create plans that were precise, and at the end of Phase 2, we sat in a room with our executives and we promised that we were 95% sure we could create the product that was mapped out in full detail in the plans on time, on budget, with the current resources, including the defined scope, and it would be at a predicted level of quality. We would all sit around the room and nod our heads in agreement that we could get this done. Our leaders would congratulate us on a great plan, and they were thrilled that we were able to reach that level of certainty.

Yet deep down, not one person in that room believed those plans. Not one person really believed that we could get the work done, or that the plan would be valid six months from then.

We need to stop having meetings where we lie to ourselves. Start to recognize these meetings, and call out that the organization needs to change. At least admit that long-term plans never happen as planned and allow the plans to be lighter weight. Start planning for change because it's going to happen.

As we have held classes and taught throughout the past decade or so, we have often asked people if they created these types of plans. Almost everyone has. When we ask how many have had the plans realized—they happened on time, on budget, with the planned scope, resources, and quality levels—no one has said yes, not one person in thousands that we have asked.

When we move toward agility, we focus on removing decisions based on false data from our business at every level. We streamline the plans and do just enough planning so we have a rough schedule and a rough budget. We think we have the right people and enough of them to get the work done based on our rough plans. Our goal is to have our plans be roughly right, because that is what they truly are, regardless of how much time we spend on them.

Back in the early 2000s there were a lot of studies done on estimation. What was the right amount of estimation to pinpoint the exact amount of work something would take to get done? Not one study came out with a method to accomplish a plan in this way. The results of these studies were that, in most instances, lightweight planning was just as accurate as detailed plans.

We'll give you an analogy to help you understand the reason behind this. Most of us commute to the office every day. We do the same commute and have for years. Knowing this, we want you to tell us the exact amount of time it will take you to get from your home to the office tomorrow to the second. You should be able to do it because it's the same commute, day after day. You've done it for years, but you can't give us an exact time frame.

Likewise, when you ask a team to come up with a schedule and plan to create a product they have never created before, how can you expect them to know exactly how much time it will take? There are far fewer variables to our work commute yet we cannot even predict that. If I ask you to detail your commute, and spend the next eight hours documenting everything about your commute that you can think of, will it make your estimate any more valid? Probably not. It will simply be a waste of your time. However, we base decisions on these types of plans every day. We force people to document things that don't get us any closer to what will really happen. We are wasting precious development dollars on these types of plans. And in the majority of cases, a percentage of this planning work is thrown out because we end up reducing scope in every release.

In the modern business, our goal is to create plans that are roughly right, not precisely wrong. In addition, that keeps us from throwing away plans for work that is never done and creating plans that don't get us any closer to a real estimate than just taking a guess (as in a plan to commute to work tomorrow).

To get back to portfolio management, your processes need to be updated to keep up with the pace of today's business. You need to think differently to work differently. Focus how you manage your portfolio and change the conversations you are having. This is fundamental to reworking your organization and being successful as you transition to focusing on value and customers rather than budgets and resources.

But Where Is My Value?

Or We've Got a Chasm II

Value created by a team is *potential value*. Nobody can use it yet. We first need to put the value somewhere that people can actually use it.

Many companies deliver their products in an on premises model. They gather the work that is done and deliver to their customers once or twice per year. This allows them to recognize revenue for those new products on the same cadence. Salespeople tend to want to sell the latest and greatest thing, which is generally what will be included in the next release. These two practices have led to more revenue recognition issues than most other business practices.

Delivering on a continuous basis helps to relieve this issue, but it's not easy to get there. We once worked with a CTO who believed if his products were "lifted and shifted" to a hosted environment that was being referred to as a "cloud" that the teams could suddenly release every month or six weeks. This just isn't the case. A lot of work needs to be done to get products, and a company, ready for continuous delivery.

© CA 2018
D. Dockery and L. Knudsen, *Modern Business Management*,
https://doi.org/10.1007/978-1-4842-3261-3_7

The Six Things Needed for Continuous Delivery

We work with companies who are making the decision to move from purely on premises delivery to full cloud delivery models. One of the most successful of these ventures was at a company that built their operations teams up while also building the infrastructure and moving all their products in the direction to be delivered on the same platform. During this process, we realized there were six main areas that needed to be modified to be successful:

- Process
- Automation
- Architecture (technology stack)
- Multitenancy
- Continuous integration and promotion
- Operations

Process

If your teams are not doing disciplined Agile practices it will take them a lot longer to be successful at delivering continuously. Teams need a continuous flow of work coming to them and fully fleshed out processes to deliver continuously. They need the right people involved at the right time.

We have seen companies that say they want to deliver continuously, yet they still force their teams through a phase gate process. Not only is the overhead burden too high on the teams, but the leadership team that has to approve all of the releases becomes too burdened when every team is releasing every month, much less if they want to release daily.

At one company, we devised a process that removed much of the overhead from the release cycle into a different cadence so that teams could deliver continuously (Figure 7-1). For example, we reviewed markets at a deep level every six months, and then on a more shallow basis the other quarters. We funded outcomes quarterly and strategies every six months.

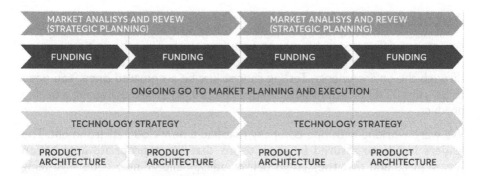

Figure 7-1. Separating process inputs from execution

We pulled architectural changes up to a similar cadence. Although we were constantly reviewing new technologies, we adopted them on a more standard cadence. This kept team disruption to a minimum, still allowing us to upgrade the tech stack, add new software capabilities (many being open source), and automate things in a planned fashion.

For each release, teams created their plan for what they were going to complete, reviewed their quality master plans to see if anything changed, and then moved forward. Leadership still wanted to see plans and results, so we moved these "gates" into a standard biweekly project review meeting we had with leadership. Generally, this meeting was to review the work in flight in our business unit to see if it was all on track. Teams who had created plans or who were ready for release reviewed the regulatory information, required plans, or release criteria and metrics instead.

We kept standard release criteria (quality levels, percentage of test cases passed, regulatory requirements complete, security sign-offs, etc.), but because there was just a small amount of code being released, we changed some of the requirements to include only delta reviews instead of the full product. We reviewed new open source being included and gained legal sign-off for the licenses, but not everything in the product. We moved these full reviews into a standard cadence (every 6–12 months depending on risk) and only reviewed the deltas for each release. If no new open source was included, no reviews were needed.

We also brought our other departments (support, marketing, sales, professional services) into the reviews so that we could keep the entire organization in sync. If you create the right processes and collaborations, you can move more quickly and not leave out any portion of your organization. The product, market, and company can be ready for every release, regardless of how quickly you distribute those releases.

Automation

You cannot deliver continuously, or even frequently, if you haven't automated the builds, the testing, and the promotion of the product, test data, and tests through the environments. Testing cannot just be automated once. You need to be using TDD or a similar technique to ensure you are delivering a quality product.

We were working with one company that had a new cloud environment. The leaders had been assured by their teams that the appropriate automation was in place and that they could deliver quickly, and all new code was being thoroughly tested. They promoted a small chunk of code through all the environments to production and a customer immediately found a severe bug. The team fixed the bug and the code was promoted through the environments and to production again, and again the customers immediately found a severe bug. This went on for three or four days with numerous fixes and promotions through all environments. As I'm sure you can guess, when we researched the root cause of the problem, it was that they did not have good processes in place to assure full automation of testing was complete and the product was not even being fully tested, because manual tests would have taken too long.

We had to slow everyone down, get the appropriate tests in place, and then implement the processes to ensure all future code had new automated tests developed, before the team was allowed to deliver quickly again. Sometimes you need to slow down in the short term to speed up in the long run.

Architecture or the Technology Stack

We don't know of many companies of size that have not purchased at least part of their product offerings. If you look at the entire product line of almost any company, each one is each created using different coding methods, different programming languages, and a different technology stack.

If you want to deliver on a cloud environment or SaaS modality, it's often highly beneficial that product lines share the same technology stack. If there are legacy products targeted for a specific cloud environment, you will want to strive to adopt as common a tech stack as possible with both new and legacy products.

At one company, we worked with a CTO who had mandated that all products would be available in an internal cloud environment. Yet when product releases were being defined, he continued to approve nonstandard technology for each product's tech stack, then wondered why it was so difficult to put new versions into production. It was taking more than 12 weeks to get some of the products available in the production environment. It often took longer to get the product into production than it did to create the next release of the product. This is a huge hit to your operation teams' productivity when you want to move products into a cloud environment and you are spending so much on getting your teams to be able to deliver continuously. Even small changes to the standard tech stack can add huge amounts of time to the actual delivery of the product into production.

Each change can break standards set up by your operations teams. If they have designed promotion schemas to move the products through environments, having a nonstandard piece in the tech stack will usually break this process. It requires manual intervention and custom automation to be created and maintained, which are all very costly. You break the repeatable processes being put in place and require each piece of software to be handled individually. In essence, you might as well not even be moving to a cloud environment.

There are more modern design principles emerging that advocate a more autonomous, decentralized, decoupled approach to building applications. Movements around domain-driven design (e.g., microservices) strive to shift some of the application complexities from the development communities to the system architects and designers. These approaches are popular and can help (particularly with new product development) but are predicated on new organizaitonal priciples (of a business domain or customer journey) and the use of modern, stateless APIs. Also emerging are more prescriptive recommendations for cloud or SaaS-specific application design (e.g., the Twelve Factor-App principles). Although these movements can help to minimize some of the challenges with a heterogeneous tech stack, even the most progressive organizations practicing these approaches recognize the value of a having a tech stack that is more similar than different. It's also important to note that these movements are focused on design and are not intended to negate the importance of good collaboration and leadership.

Choosing the right platform (or choosing to create portable components independent of platforms) and requiring all teams to follow design guidelines is important as you work toward continuous delivery.

Multitenancy

Usually, a product that is sold for an on premises delivery is meant to be used by one customer. It is installed within the firewalls of the company that purchased the product and is used solely by them.

When products are in a cloud or SaaS environment, they are meant to be used by more than one customer at the same time. One of the goals of a cloud environment, and one of the main benefits, is having only one instance of the software to be maintained. Let's just say there is a lot of work that needs to be done to allow more than one customer into the same instance of a product and to ensure the security of each customer's data. This is often something that takes months of work to complete and even longer to test.

You can't rush this step. It is up to your application's design and architecture to keep the data secure, not the cloud platform. Be sure you understand all regulations for storing the customers' data and make sure your multitenancy schemes are fully tested. One defect that allows a customer to view other customers' data can cause your product to fail and your company to become an untrusted entity by your users. Plan this out prior to moving software into a SaaS or cloud environment.

Continuous (Frequent) Integration and Promotion

In the old days of software development, each developer would check out code from the source control repository and complete all work on that code before they checked it back in. This created a nightmare of integration every few weeks or months when the integrations of all the developers' code was checked in. We remember it taking up to six weeks to integrate the code and do an initial test cycle.

It's a good thing those days are gone. Now we expect integrations to occur much more frequently. On the path to continuous delivery, many companies are now integrating continuously or at the very least a few times per day. Many integrate at set times throughout the day and everyone must check in their code before the set times. Other companies integrate every time code is checked in to the source repository. In the early days of XP, continuous integration was intended to be used in combination with automated unit tests and the practice of TDD. All unit tests would be run in the developer's environment and all unit tests would need to pass before the code was committed to the repository. This helps to avoid one developer's work breaking another developer's copy.

Today, many environments include a test server or build server where the integrations are more fully tested prior to being committed to the source code repository. These processes usually are part of a broader quality management system and often include running integration tests, static and dynamic tests, usability tests, performance tests, and scalability tests.

Operations Teams

The previous five areas are usually where the development teams need to focus. In addition to this, the operations group needs to build up three areas:

- *DevOps (development operations):* These are the people that automate the processes used to move a product successfully through the environments.

- *ProdOps (production operations):* These are the people who are responsible for the production environment and all that is in it. In regulated environments, only those in ProdOps can access the production environment.

- *ServiceOps (service operations):* These are the new support groups that are needed to support the SaaS or cloud environment. They are in addition to the support organization that supports the products.

Today, these three areas are often all referred to as DevOps, but they generally have different skill sets and focus on meeting different goals.

DevOps? We Don't Need No DevOps

The operations teams generally own the environments that come after engineering and QA through production. Depending on regulatory requirements and the types of products you are delivering to your customers, there can be many stages (Figure 7-2). For example:

- *Integration testing:* All software running together on one platform. These products might actually work together or just need to run on the same servers.

- *Performance testing:* Ensuring all software runs at appropriate levels and speed.

- *Security validation:* Often verified with scanning software. Ensures there are no security holes in the updated software.

- *Usability testing:* Validated standards are followed and users have a good experience with your product; it is intuitive.

- *Customer staging:* If customers can configure or customize your products, there is often an environment where they can test the new applications.

- *Customer testing:* In some regulated environments and with mission-critical products, customers are provided a place to validate updates prior to moving them into production.

- *Preproduction (OAT or ORT):* Final internal testing is done to ensure all products work together. This environment mimics production as closely as possible, and if a product does not pass tests, it is reverted to the previous version. Products are either promoted to production or reverted immediately.

- *Production:* The products are live and available for customers to use.

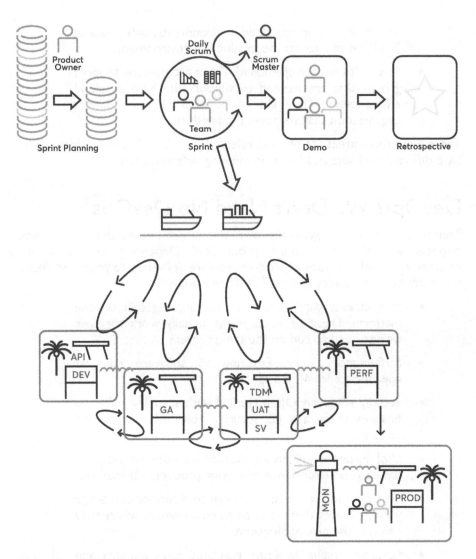

Figure 7-2. Delivering in a cloud or SaaS environment

These environments make up a portion of your entire quality management system and software releases flow through them. The more automated the promotion of releases through these environments, along with smoke tests and test data, the easier it is for you to release continuously. Make sure you have tools that allow you to push not only the updated software, but automated tests and test data between the environments. Optimally, the tool should also notify a specified group of people if there is a problem.

There are regulations in many industries regarding who can have access to each environment, when they can have access, and how it must be controlled. There are requirements for error and processing logs, monitoring of environments and environmental stability, and time frames to fix errors. Be sure to fully understand all regulations required for your products and markets and incorporate those into your standard processes.

Beyond DevOps

As we've mentioned before, continuous delivery of products, whether you can truly release continuously or whether you begin to release much more frequently (one-month or six-week increments is common), is one of the tipping points that requires agility to move into additional parts of your organization. Can your sales people sell in six-week increments rather than large, big bang releases? Do your release numbering schemes still work?

Software releases used to be called major, minor, maintenance, and patch (or service pack, or something similar). Numbering schemes went with each one, often using decimal points to indicate the next level of release. When you release every six weeks, these release types no longer fit. Generally, people are giving their releases a number that corresponds to the month and year, or year and release number for that year.

When you move toward continuous delivery you will need to rework all company processes and policies to align with the new release cadence. Hopefully you can streamline them as well. Make sure your support staff can support the releases, your sales and marketing people understand how to market and sell the new functionality, and you might even need to rework your product numbers for contracts.

Moving to continuous delivery requires change on a larger scale than just your development teams. It is a catalyst for broad-scale changes throughout your organization. It presents a great opportunity to review all aspects of your organization and to modify and update them to align to modern business practices.

True Transformation Equals Value

From Planning to Use

Annual planning is still done in most organizations. How much planning is done, and whether the plans are roughly right or precisely wrong is the key to pulling agility into the strategic and annual planning processes.

Portions of the annual plan need to be roll-ups of the detailed team plans and others need to flow from the top level down into the teams. Let's look at which plans flow in each direction and determine who needs detailed information and who needs summary information.

Resource Management

People want to be seen as individuals on teams, so referring to them as resources, staff, or titles and numbers feels degrading. However, we still need to understand how many people with specific skills we need so we can ensure we match the number of people in our organization to budgets. Traditionally this has been called resource allocation or resource management.

© CA 2018
D. Dockery and L. Knudsen, *Modern Business Management*,
https://doi.org/10.1007/978-1-4842-3261-3_8

So how do we do this? Determine the level of detail you need at each level of your organization, as shown in Table 8-1. While your managers and directors need to make sure they have the right individuals with the right skill sets on their teams, the group that does annual planning generally does not.

Level	Role
Manager	Understand each person on the team by name, their competency (skill + knowledge), aptitude (ability to learn), passion (desire to do what they do), and engagement level. Determine how many teams you need to meet strategic goals.
Director	Understand specific numbers and skills needed on each team they oversee, and how those skills align to pay bands. Ensure correct people are on each team and agree on number of teams needed to meet strategic goals.
Vice president	Within their product lines, understand number of people needed at each pay band level and be able to defend why they are needed with data (both current staffing and demands for new hires). Align market size with future plans and ensure staffing level requests are warranted. Combine team plans with full plan for all resources needed to maintain product line such as marketing, product management, operations, and so on, that are not included in the team plans.
Finance	How many people at each level and in each job, can we afford? How many do we need? How many are being requested?
C-Level/EPMO	Understand resource needs at each pay band across all product lines. Understand market sizing and corporate strategy and initiatives and how product lines align to them. Ensure full team plans exist at lower levels. Understand full resource needs against product lines for profit and loss plans.

Figure 8-1 shows what this might look like.

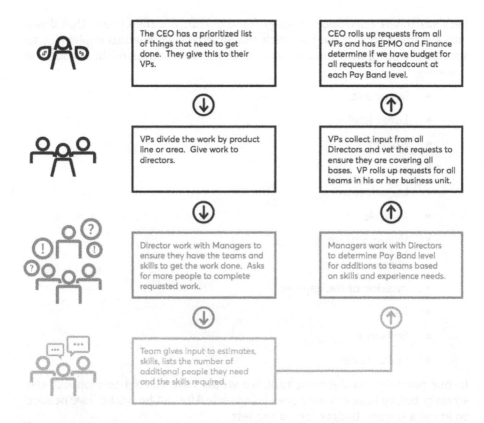

The CEO has a prioritized list of things that need to get done. They give this to their VPs.

CEO rolls up requests from all VPs and has EPMO and Finance determine if we have budget for all requests for headcount at each Pay Band level.

VPs divide the work by product line or area. Give work to directors.

VPs collect input from all Directors and vet the requests to ensure they are covering all bases. VP rolls up requests for all teams in his or her business unit.

Director work with Managers to ensure they have the teams and skills to get the work done. Asks for more people to complete requested work.

Managers work with Directors to determine Pay Band level for additions to teams based on skills and experience needs.

Team gives input to estimates, skills, lists the number of additional people they need and the skills required.

Figure 8-1. General resource management

At the top level, you should no longer need all the details you had previously. If you flow work to teams, instead of forming teams to do the work, you will know each team's capacity, their skills, and how they work. Let's look at this using an example we might all be familiar with.

Man to the Moon

In May 1961, John F Kennedy gave a pretty famous speech. He was asking for funding for a major initiative: landing a man on the moon and returning him safely to earth. If you review the speech, it fulfills everything generally asked in today's business cases: It started with the why (freedom over tyranny) and it included differentiators, why we believe we can meet these goals, and what will happen if we don't.

Let's start with this: Our mission is to land a man on the moon and bring him safely back to earth. Very little of the technology existed in 1961 to make this project a reality. It was forging new ground in almost every arena, and it was a huge project.

Let's say this is our major strategy for the year. We then break that down into initiatives so that we can track the initiatives we need to implement to successfully put a man on the moon. Our list of initiatives might include the following:

- Space suit
- Lunar lander
- Rocket
- Food
- Launch tower
- Capsule
- Water system
- Mission control
- Interior of the capsule
- Fuel
- Software
- Lunar rover

In our portfolio management tool, we would have started to map out this strategy before Kennedy ever gave his speech. After all, he would have needed to know a starting budget for his request.

We would enter each of these areas into our portfolio management tool as a project. We would start to build out what each of these projects would take. In 1961, we knew nothing about space or how it would affect a human, so we had to guess at the types of engineers we would need and how many of them would be needed. Software wasn't really a thing yet, so it wasn't like you could go out and hire 500 software developers.

They still needed to come up with a budget though. They made educated guesses. They based the rocket build on rockets that were made to shoot missiles. They extrapolated data and made guesses about other types of people they would would need. They created a "resource plan" and a capital expense total, and applied budgetary data, and came up with an initial budgetary ask.

Then, Kennedy gave his speech asking for the money. It was approved.

Each of these initiatives will be tracked as a project in our portfolio management tool and each will have teams—some will have really large teams—to complete these projects. They will all be expensive, but Kennedy had received funding for the project. Governance would start on the project as we start to break down the work and we look at how we want data to flow back up to give us a good status of the project.

If we look at the resources that existed at NASA, they had rocket scientists because they were creating missiles. Some of the teams that were creating missiles could be repurposed to work on the rockets. In a fully Agile environment, the work would flow to the scientists. Other teams would need to be hired in or outsourced.

We need to be able to track the work that goes into each of these projects, and in an Agile environment, we would next break these initiatives down into features. Features are a really important part of the work breakdown because they are something that everyone can understand. They should be written in such a way that anyone can read them and get an idea of what is being created.

- Executives should be able to read them and understand how they fit into the initiative.

- Customers should be able to read them and understand what they will be getting and they should see value in them.

- The execution teams, who will be creating the product day after day, should be able to read them and see how their piece of work fits into the whole.

In this project, let's break down the space suit. For the suit, we would have things like these, shown in Figure 8-2:

- Helmet
- Gloves
- Arm assembly
- Communication assembly
- Battery
- Primary life support system
- Secondary oxygen pack
- Drink bag

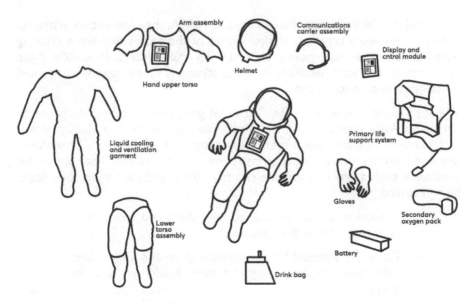

Figure 8-2. Space suit components

This is where we bring all the teams that will be working on the space suit into one room and share with them our ideas and high-level requirements for the suit. It needs to hold air in, it needs to protect the astronauts from radiation, and it needs to allow them to still move and complete tasks. They cannot overheat, and so on. Everyone hears about the basic requirements and goals for the project, and then these teams go back and start creating stories for their feature.

At this time, we want to define working agreements and our agreed-on definition of done. A definition of done is a list of things everyone agrees must be complete for a story to be considered fully complete. It includes things like whether unit testing needs to be complete, whether the acceptance criteria need to all be met, if code is checked in to source control, and if documentation needs to be done. Many companies include things like zero defects open, meaning that every defect found during the iteration must be closed before a story can be considered complete. Other defects might be found during further tests, but everything found during the iteration must be closed.

Now let's say we're part of the glove team as they break down their work into user stories. User stories, when following best practice, are generally no more than three to four days of work, which includes engineering and test time. Each story has acceptance criteria, which let the developer and the QA folks know when the story is done. User stories for gloves might include the following:

- As an astronaut, I want a glove that allows me to pick up and use tools so I can accomplish tasks.

- As an astronaut, I want a glove that is tear resistant, so my blood does not boil.

- As an astronaut, I want a glove that allows as much dexterity as possible, so I can drive and use tools.

- As an astronaut, I want a nonporous glove so I am not contaminated with space goo.

You get the picture. The work is broken down until each user story can be completed within a few days. If the estimate on the story is too high, we break that story into two stories. We want to be able to move items to the "done" pile as quickly as possible.

The detail is amazing in Agile projects. You can see the design emerge. This is not to say that there is no up-front design in Agile projects. Design documents can be done when they make sense, but we no longer believe mapping things out to the level of a detailed specification provides us much value.

Teams work on breaking down their features into user stories as much as possible until the two-day period when we hold our big room planning. The stories are prioritized so the teams know what to work on first.

Everyone participates: every member of every execution team, system teams, executives needed for trade-off decisions, business partners, and so on. If there are dependencies on other teams, those teams are also represented. In this two-day period, the final stories are fleshed out; capacity plans are set; dependencies are tracked; risks are removed, mitigated, or accepted; and trade-off decisions are made by leadership. In traditional projects, getting to this level of planning takes weeks, if not months. At some companies, we never understand all the dependencies until things don't work together. This planning meeting, although expensive, is one of the most valuable things you can do as an organization to move your company forward.

Either during the big room planning or right after, some teams break the stories down into tasks, which are no more than one day of work. Think of every team doing this type of breakdown structure. Every person who will be involved in completing the projects to get us to space has been breaking down their features into stories. The stories have been prioritized and those that will be done in the first three months are broken down completely to no more than four days of work, and are ready to be started. The remainder of the work can stay at a higher level of planning because we aren't ready to work on it yet.

Each group has had its two-day big room planning session. Each has discussed its design and has release plans complete. The sheer level of detail, which we never had before, is remarkable.

Now teams start doing the work. They begin their iterations, make their final commitments for their two-week sprints or iterations, and complete their work. Every story that is moved into the completed state meets the agreed-on definition of done, and meets the acceptance criteria for that user story. All defects are closed. The definition of done might include things like all tasks are completed, acceptance criteria have been met, all defects are closed, unit tests are complete, code reviews are done, automated tests are implemented, and development documentation is complete.

As a leader, have you ever had this much information about the status of your projects before? When someone said they were done, did you have to ask qualifying questions? Could you look at a status chart and know, with certainty, that the work was done to an agreed-on level of quality? This is one of the most valuable ways in which Agile practices benefit an organization and the executive team specifically. Using this technique of breaking down work and having standards in place, you can see where every development dollar is going. You can see the day-to-day status of every piece of work in your organization. You can see the value being created against your strategies. The days of relying on biweekly verbal status meetings are over. This is the age of big data—inside your organization.

Let's think about who needs this level of data that we are amassing. If all the work is broken down into pieces of no more than three days, that is a lot of details. Who needs these data? The President certainly didn't need all of these details. He would be overwhelmed.

The head of the space suit project probably didn't need this level of detail either. He or she needed a higher level view into the work and generally only needs details if a team is falling behind or going over budget.

The leader of the teams creating the pieces of the space suit certainly needed it, though. The development team for the glove certainly needed it. The people creating the other parts of the space suit might find value in some of the data as well. For example, if the glove team is the first one to test a textile to ensure it limits radiation exposure, other teams might not need to do the same test.

As the teams complete their work, we roll up the data for each part of the suit:

- Gloves = 10% complete
- Helmet = 7% complete
- Boots = 12% complete
- Drink bag = 100% complete

Now who needs this type of information? As you go up the management chain, each level needs fewer details unless an issue starts to arise. Then they dig in, but still only to a certain level. With all that data in your Agile life cycle management tool, you have real-time status on every part of the work being done.

This is the big internal data that we talked about earlier. It's a next revolution in work management and will be the basis of Artificial Intelligence (AI) in the future. You need this today to manage and steer your organization to compete in today's fast-paced markets. AI will need this data to help you plan better, report on exact status, show you what is happening in your organization. If you don't have this data consistently managed for all teams, you will fall behind your competition.

On the other hand, if you are letting your teams choose the tools they use to manage their work—also known as your development dollars—then you are creating a pile of junk data. Inconsistent teams with inconsistent data and workflows will give you a pile of garbage data. You might be collecting lots and lots of data but all it equates to is a landfill of junk. Work-tracking data must be consistent to get a realistic view into the execution against these plans and to pass audits.

If teams are:

- using different platforms (we like to allow development teams to choose their own tools)
- allowed to set up work items differently (fields in stories, defects, test cases)
- allowed to use a platform in an inconsistent fashion (creating their own workflows and primary data fields)

then you won't have a reliable view into the status of your projects, nor will you have reliable traceability. If your competition has these data and you don't, you will lose.

If you have integrated portfolio management systems with your Agile life cycle management tool, you can roll up all this wonderful data and see the overall status.

In your portfolio management tool, you can track the percentage of the budget that has been spent to make sure we can cover the entire project. Generally, we look at Cap Ex vs. Op Ex, whether teams are dedicated or being pulled off onto other projects, and together all of these data show whether the project is on time.

This gives you complete insight into the day-to-day status of every strategy you have set. It shows you value being created against your strategies and initiatives. When a disruptor hits your market, or you come up with an idea to become the disruptor, you can easily see which teams are available to flow work to without interrupting your current strategies.

With disciplined Agile methods, you can have real-time status of all work being done, unlike what we had when we based our project progress on verbal input given at a biweekly meeting.

Using these data, you can ensure you are creating the most value for your company, aligning your teams to the most profitable and cost-efficient work. When new ideas or market disruptions arise, you can see which teams have completed the most value against their initiatives and strategies and flow the new work to those teams, ensuring your current strategies will still provide the value you predicted. Using these data is the only way to ensure you can keep up with fast-changing markets and disruptions we see today.

Funding

Many companies fund their business units or product lines on an annual basis. They review the market requirement documents or business cases and determine a chunk of funding to provide to each organization. This funding drives the number of teams they can have and how much work can get done.

Many people are talking about moving to incremental funding. That sounds good, but what does that really mean? Most companies are not equipped to complete their funding processes multiple times per year. Doing it once in a year generally takes two to three months. So how will they accomplish it multiple times per year?

The goal of incremental funding is to be able to respond to the market as it changes. If you have a business that covers multiple markets, as most of us do, then we need to respond to the changes happening in every market. Hopefully we are not just responding, but are the frontrunners in our markets. We should be the disruptors. We need to have money to be able to steer our company as new ideas hit us or as the markets change, or new competition rears its head.

There are a few ways you can do this. We've seen companies being successful by running their annual funding but only allocating 75% to 80% of their budget to the various business units. The remainder is allocated as needed to meet changing market needs or to develop new ideas.

Other companies are funding their business units, but allow the leaders to determine how to spend the money throughout the year. Of course, they have goals and strategies when they allocate the funding, but if something comes up that would allow a business unit to capture more market value or disrupt their market then they can change how they spend their money without further approvals. This push requires the leaders of each business unit to be accountable for producing the value that the company needs, based on the allocation of funds they were given.

If something dramatically changes in the markets, organizations are replanning and reallocating the money. They pull it from one business unit and give it to another.

Some companies are still doing their funding on an annual basis, but they have implemented a planned "replanning period" halfway through the fiscal year. They are thus essentially doing a minifunding process halfway through the year. They also then lighten up the annual process because they know they will revisit it in six months.

The main goal of these various methods is to be able to respond to the market. As we have mentioned previously, streamlining the processes at every level—even annual planning—allows you to make these changes to how you do business and to align your business processes to modern business practices.

How Do You Know It's Working?

Because you know that the goal of an Agile business is a continuing journey and not a destination, let's take a look at how our processes might align when things are working more efficiently and effectively.

Predictability

All teams should be predictable. If you plan during a big room planning style of meeting then you have a planned scope for the next three months. This scope should stay stable, even if a new requirement is added because a requirement of equal value must be removed from the scope. Remember, teams plan to capacity so they can work to a sustainable pace. Teams at full capacity cannot have work added without removing something of equal value.

If your teams have planned well, and they understand their own capacity, then they quickly become predictable. We used to tell our teams that they didn't have to estimate well, just consistently poorly. We can apply a modifier to help them understand their capacity.

D. Dockery and L. Knudsen, *Modern Business Management*,
https://doi.org/10.1007/978-1-4842-3261-3_9

One way to get teams to a predictable state is to watch how well they meet their sprint commitments. We used to watch any team that didn't meet their commitment at the end of the first sprint. If they didn't meet their commitment at the end of their second sprint, we would contact them to see if there was a reason or if they were struggling to meet the planned scope. At the end of the third sprint, if they again didn't meet the commitment, we would ask them to replan their work.

This allowed us to see within two or three sprints that a release was not going to be done as planned. It also helped the team to get to an understanding of their true velocity.

We know from experience that "driving" the team to meet their committed scope rather than allowing them to replan will have a very poor outcome. Quality suffers greatly, as does morale and, in the long run, so does productivity. It's better to replan early and reset expectations rather than drive a team past what it can reasonably accomplish.

Objective Decision Making

Using the data from our Agile prjects allows us to make decisions objectively rather than influenced by how we feel about the work being done.

We were working with a large equipment manufacturer and the first wave of the transformation was complete. The leadership went before their funding board to request the money needed for the second wave. The funding board asked how it was going. Our executive sponsor answered that it felt like it was going well. Needless to say, no additional budget was given.

We had to go back and pull the Agile coaches away from teams to gather information so that we could present something more definitive than what it felt like to the funding board.

Transforming an entire organization can't be based on how we feel. In the previous chapter we showed you the rich data that you should be getting from your Agile execution teams, and as you move agility through your entire business, from all teams doing any work in your organization. No longer do we need to base decisions on how someone feels a project is progressing. We can know the value being created and exactly what has been done.

How do you make decisions in your organization? If they aren't based on real data, how do you know it's the right decision?

Agile Metrics

We need to have the ability to create metrics from our Agile data that all levels of an organization can see and use. This requires standard data and workflows among all teams.

When we have been engaged by a new company to start their Agile transformation, the first thing we would ask—from the C-level through directors—is what data they want to see to run their business.

Some people know exactly what they like to see, whereas others have no idea and ask what they should be using. Every person running a substantial portion of a business (generally directors and above) need good, solid data to be able to run their business day-to-day and to steer the business when change is needed.

Change is usually needed when a competitor hits the market with a disruption, or you determine a way you can disrupt the market, or the market has a new need. If someone is going to disrupt your market, shouldn't it be you?

If you know what your teams are working on, and how far along they are in the value they are creating, you can use these data to make the decision on the best team(s) to flow new work to. If you don't have real, consistent data, you are blind to the impact of the changes you make.

This isn't to say that every team has to do everything the exact same way. That is surely not Agile. However, there should be standard workflows and a subset of standard data for each work unit (feature, story, defect, test case, test result) so that you can get standard reporting. Outside of those standard fields, the teams can do whatever they want.

What metrics does your organization use to measure success? Are they the right ones? How do you know? Can you see where every development and IT dollar is being spent? Why not? Do you have the data to successfully steer your organization? What if your competition does?

Cumulative Flow Diagram

From my experience, the cumulative flow diagram with a trend line is one of the best you can use to see project status (Figure 9-1).

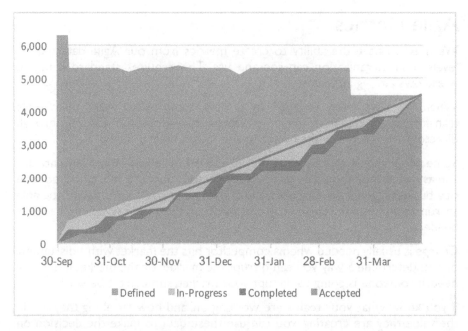

Figure 9-1. Cumulative flow: Sample 1

The orange area (top) is the scope. You can see it varied at the very beginning of the project during planning, then it was relatively stable as we went through the project. The team needed to adjust their scope approximately six weeks prior to their release date (which could have been done much earlier because we could see by the trend line that they were not going to make it). However, this team reduced scope because they created enough value. We were able to end the project early and eliminate features that people decided they no longer needed.

When was the last time you were able to end a project early because you knew you had created the desired outcome? This team was able to take on other, unplanned work that created even more value for customers.

The yellow area (upper middle) represents work in progress. This team did well with not taking on too much at once and consistently finishing what they started.

The blue area (lower middle) represents completed work. You want this area to be as small as possible because work should not sit in complete status without being accepted. Stairsteps in this area show that the team might not be breaking their user stories down small enough (everything completing at the end of an iteration vs. throughout).

The green area (bottom) is accepted work. There is a stairstep to this as well, which usually indicates that the product owner is not as engaged with the team as they should be. However, because this green aligns pretty well with the blue, this is not the case here.

With a second example (Figure 9-2), you can see the scope is erratic. It is not planned properly and you need to investigate what is going on with this work.

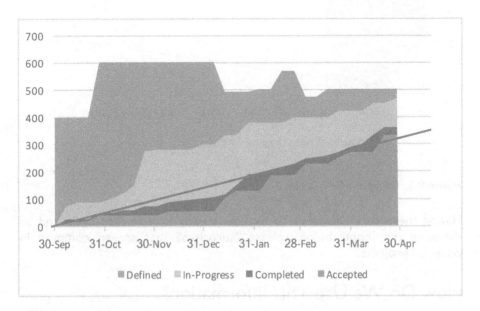

Figure 9-2. Cumulative flow: Sample 2

There is also much too much work in progress (WiP). The team will not be completing items efficiently because they are taking on too much at once. Coach the team to limit WiP.

Work is waiting in a completed state before it is being accepted and there are times when the product owner is not engaged with the team (large stairstep in the green area). You can see from the trend line (diagonal green line) that this team has planned too much scope and will probably not complete the project on time. You can make the decision regarding whether to push out the date or reduce scope early in this project.

In a third example (Figure 9-3) you can see early on in the project that the estimations are not realistic. After just a couple of iterations, you can see that it's time to replan the entire project and make the plan realistic. The trend line shows the team will complete less than half of the work that is currently planned for the project.

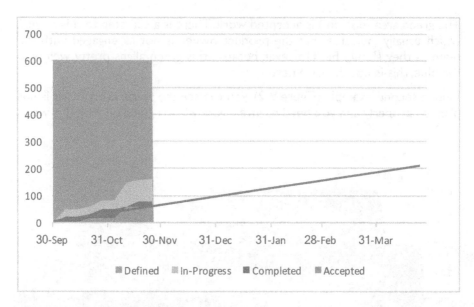

Figure 9-3. Cumulative flow: Sample 3

Having these data allows us to fix issues early in a release cycle and to eliminate the month-before-release "surprises" that are so common in waterfall projects.

How Do We Use This Information?

This one chart can give every level of your organization the information they need to see the status of every project and to see where every dollar is being spent.

It's one metric you can use as a standard to know a project's status. We generally put guidelines around how we coach teams using the cumulative flow diagram.

If teams working on a project or release miss their commitments for their first iterations (teams working on the same product or release should have aligned iteration cadences; e.g., all start on the same Monday and end on the same Friday), we start watching them. If they again miss their commitment for the second iterations, we contact the team leaders to see if they believe they can recover or if the project is already so far out of plan that the teams cannot meet their initial plan. If the teams believe they can recover, we give them one or two additional iterations and then replan the release if they are not back on track.

This allows us to make sure we have realistic plans in place and we have a pretty good understanding of what we can deliver very early in our release cycles. It gives leadership more predictable projects, based on real data instead of verbal status, and it helps teams to understand how much work they can actually get done so we eliminate the "pie in the sky" plans.

By doing this we start running our business based on real data. We talk about realities instead of showing a green status that was done verbally. The impact of this on the leadership's ability to steer the organization, and on the program-level trade-off decisions that often need to be made when the unforeseen risk occurs, is incredible.

Now imagine if you had these data for every project in your organization, and you could see that quickly what was actually going to be delivered and what value was going to be created against every one of your corporate strategies. This is the power of good Agile practices and data.

So, When Will We Be Done?

Well, let's see. When will your business be done? When will the main product you sell be done? When will you sit back and say, "That's it! That's all we can do as a company"? At that point, you're done.

It's a Journey, Not a Destination

If you haven't made continuous improvement part of your everyday vocabulary, then you need to start today. Your path to better efficiency, to better ways of running every aspect of your company, should never end. We have worked with companies who believe they have completed their journey to agility so they stop looking at their internal processes and procedures. They lay off the people who they hired to get them to their new way of working or they don't replace them when those folks move on. Within months, the company starts to lose ground.

It would be akin to believing you have the best technology stack for your product line so you allow all your architects to leave. How long would it take your product to be out of date?

There will always be something that happens, whether internal or external to your company, that causes a need for change to occur. You can always improve every aspect of your business. Ten years ago, people weren't talking about cloud environments, yet now you hear that phrase a lot. There will always be changes to technology and new innovations that require us to look at how we run our businesses and how we work together. Using new methods and taking advantage of the data that are created is a great way to move your company forward.

What's Next for Agile?

We started with Thiel's brilliant question: "What important truth do very few people agree with you on?" What important truth will your Agile organization discover and how will you use that to create value now and in the future?

Le Agile est mort, vive le Agile?

Agile means doing things in a way that makes the most sense. Take into consideration all you know and what your instincts are telling you and look at how your company can be more efficient, effective, and smart.

The future of Agile is that it will become the norm. All of these practices and principles become what we do without needing to be taught. The principles will move into every part of our businesses and in the way we interact with other companies, and with each other.

Bringing Agile into every part of our business allows us to steer even the largest organizations to respond to market changes, disruptions, and competitors. We will no longer talk about transitioning to Agile methodologies because this will be how everyone works—regardless of industry. Colleges have been teaching agility as the way to create products for years now.

The principles of Agile will continue to permeate every area of our businesses. Industries that are not being touched today (e.g., some financial firms and law firms) will move toward using similar principles. Regardless of what we are creating and where it is being made, or what type of work we are doing, we will work in small batches with more frequent check-ins, more collaboration, and more transparency.

Data will continue to be one of the most valuable resources we have and will continue to be the way the world tracks and measures us. Data that show what is happening *inside* your company are becoming just as important as big data is for external customers. You will need to understand how much value your teams are creating day by day to ensure you are keeping up with the competition. As AI is developed, having data about what is happening inside of your organization will become just as important as customer data. Start collecting data now so that when AI and machine learning is added to your current products, you can benefit immediately.

We believe that the term *Agile* will be dropped from our vocabulary in the next few years and that these techniques, methods, and practices will become modern business management.

I

Index

A

Activity-based accounting, 111

Ad-hoc feedback, 37

Adoption, effect on, 46

Agenda for meeting, 82

Agile
definition, 1, 27
development, 28
future of, 152
lean adoption, 17
methods
design thinking, 15
extreme programming (XP), 13
Kanban, 13
lean principles, 14–15
lean start up, 15
scrum, 12–13
metrics, 147
practices
benefits to executives, 16
uses, 15–16
principles of, 152
value, focus on, 2

Agile concepts, framework, 83, 85
product life cycles, 83
product management professionals, 83

Agile manifesto, 2
customer collaboration, 4
for software development, 1
individuals and interactions, 3
principles, 5, 7–11
responding to change, 4

values, 2
working software, 4

Agile quantified, impact of, 49
benefit of dedicated teams, 50
productivity, 52
quality, 51, 54
responsiveness, 53
retrospectives and performance, 55
scrum estimation processes, 50

Annual planning, 67, 133
invest in right things, 68–69
prioritization by value, 69

B

Backlogs, 42–43, 78

Big room planning, 82

Business transformation, failure modes, 18
checkbook commitments, 20
decentralizing control, failure of, 30–34
executive leadership, lack of, 18–19
checkbook commitments, 20
skunk works, 19
fast feedback, failure to create, 36–37
focus on people, failure to, 40
organizational structure, 24–26
path of Individual, ignoring, 40, 42
shortchanging collaboration and
facilitation, 37–38
transformation product manager,
lack of, 34–35
transform beyond IT, failure to, 38–39
transforming leader behavior, 20–22
values, 28–29

© CA 2018
D. Dockery and L. Knudsen, *Modern Business Management*,
https://doi.org/10.1007/978-1-4842-3261-3

Business transformation, failure modes (*cont.*)
    work from backlogs, failure to, 42–43
    work practice, 26–28

C

CA value delivery model, 84
Chasm, 71
    framework for crossing, 76
        method, 76, 78, 80
Chief information security
        officer (CISO), 103
Consultants, to solve problems, 73
Continuous delivery
    automation, 126
    continuous integration and
        promotion, 128
    multitenancy, 127–128
    operation teams, 128
    process, 124–125
    technology, 126–127
Control
    eliminating distributed teams, 33–34
    pivots, 30
    product development flow, 30–33
Cumulative flow diagram, 147
    sample, 148–150

D

Data, valuable resource, 152
Dependencies, 82
DevOps, 110, 129
    cloud or SaaS environment, delivering, 130
    regulations, 131
    rework on process and policy, 131
    stages in product delivery, 129

E

Executive leadership, 18–19
    checkbook commitment, 20
    skunk work, 19

F

Fast feedback, 36–37
Five Dysfunctions of a Team, The, 38

Four-phase process, 102
Funding
    annual basis, 143
    incremental, 142

G

Globalization *vs.* innovation, 45

H

House of Lean, 105
    flow, 107
    innovation, 107
    leadership, 108
    relentless improvement, 107
    respect for people and
        culture, 106
    value, 106
Human resources
    systems of collaboration, 114
    transparency, 114

I, J

Individual, path of, 40–41
Information
    data, 91
    for doing job, 90
    use of, 150–151
Innovation, 45, 48, 107

K

Kubler-Ross change curve, 40

L

Leader behavior, transformation
    commitments to team, 21
    planning, 22
    principles, 22–24
Lean accounting, 111
    definition and use, 112
    value of, 112–113
        costs, 113
        customer value, 112
Lean or Agile transformations, 48
Legacy *vs.* Lean thinking, 118

M, N

Managing dependencies and skill
        constraints, 79

Man to the Moon (sample), 135
    Agile environment, 137
    budget, 136
    data, 140, 142
    initiatives, 136
    mission, 135
    planning session, 140
    portfolio management tool, 136
    to break down the space suit, 137
    user stories, 139
    work agreements, 138

Marketing
    Agile, 116
    campaigns, 116
    digital, 116
    teams, 116

Minimum viable product (MVP) and
        iteration, 46–47

O

Objective decision making, 146

Organizational structure, 24
    goals, 25
    metrics, 25
    work appraisal, 26

Organization, Lean and
        Agile in, 108
    DevOps area, 109
    infrastructure change, 110
    phases, agile adoption, 108
    planning and integration, 109
    portfolio planning, 109
    products, 109
    scrum, 110
    transformation, 109

P, Q

People, focus on, 40

Phases, 91–92
    change management, 94
    governance, 94
    process, 92

Platform, 85–86
    proving value, 88
    value, 86

Portfolio and program management
    Agile practices, 116
    planning, 119–120
    PMO office, 117
    strategy, 119

Portfolio management, 136

Potential value, 123

Predictability, 145–146

Prioritizations, 87

Process, to solve problems, 73

ProdOps, 110

"Product development flow", 30–31, 33

R

Regulation, key areas, 92
    change management, 94–95
    documentation, 92–93
    governance, 94

Regulatory information, 90

Resource management, 133, 135

Risks, 82

S

Sales
    leadership, 115
    long sales cycle, 115
    teams, 116

Scrum, 27

Shortchanging collaboration and
        facilitation, 37–38

Skunk works, 19

Stack-rank method, 87

Standard four-phase product life cycle, 103

Strategy and execution
    commonsense approach to connecting, 81
    disconnected, 72

Streamlined life cycle
    delivery, 100
    development, 99–100

Streamlined life cycle (*cont.*)
    market validation, 95–96
    planning, 97
        gate/milestone, 99
    post release, 101
    streamline regulatory
        requirements, 103
Streamlined product life cycle, 90
    data required, 91
    information for doing job, 90
    regulatory information, 90
Streamline regulatory requirements,
    103–104
Success, framework for, 74
    frame, definition, 76
    people, 75–76

T, U

Team, information about, 57
    daily standups, 63
    iteration or sprint, 61
    organization, 58
    people assigned to product owner/
        scrum master roles, 62–63
    questions, 58
    requirements document, 59
    sprint review (Demo), 63
    values, delivery of, 60–61

    working from backlog, 59–60
    work practice, 59
Test-driven development (TDD)
        techniques, 91
Three simple questions
    annual planning, 67, 69–70
    team, information about, 57
    workflow in organization, 64–66
Tool, to solve problems, 73
Traditional accounting, 111
Transfomation triangle, 74
Transformation beyond IT, 38–39

V

Values, 28–29
    continuous delivery, 123
    potential, 123
    proving, 88–89

W, X, Y, Z

Weighted shortest job first (WSJF), 87
Work flow in organization
    backlogs, estimation of, 65
    backlogs, order of, 64
    planning, 65–66
    team-level execution, 67

Get the eBook for only $5!

Why limit yourself?

With most of our titles available in both PDF and ePUB format, you can access your content wherever and however you wish—on your PC, phone, tablet, or reader.

Since you've purchased this print book, we are happy to offer you the eBook for just $5.

To learn more, go to http://www.apress.com/companion or contact support@apress.com.

Apress®

Lightning Source UK Ltd.
Milton Keynes UK
UKHW02f1620230118
316702UK00006B/110/P